Sounding the Whale

Sounding the Whale

Moby-Dick as Epic Novel

Christopher Sten

The Kent State University Press

Kent, Ohio, & London, England

Library of Congress Catalog Card Number 96-17392
ISBN 0-87338-560-8
Manufactured in the United States of America

03 02 01 00 99 98 97 96 5 4 3 2 1

Library of Congress Cataloging-in-Publication Data

Sten, Christopher, 1944–
Sounding the whale : Moby-Dick as epic novel / Christopher Sten.
p. cm.
Previously published as ch. 6 of The weaver God, he weaves. Kent, Ohio : Kent State University Press, 1996. With a new introd.
Includes bibliographical references and index.
ISBN 0-87338-560-8 (pbk : alk. paper) ∞
1. Melville, Herman, 1819–1891. Moby-Dick. 2. Epic literature, American—History and criticism. 3. Sea stories, American—History and criticism. 4. Whaling in literature. 5. Whales in literature. I. Sten, Christopher, 1944–. Weaver-God, he weaves. II. Title.
PS2384.M62S69 1996
813′.3—dc20 96-17392

British Library Cataloging-in-Publication data are available.

Contents

Preface

As a quest epic, *Moby-Dick* is Melville's most ambitious novel, and his most challenging. As such, it requires the most careful and responsive reading imaginable. But care and responsiveness, good Ishmaelian virtues though they are, are likely to take one only so far into the labyrinth of *The Whale*. For a clear apprehension of the intricacy and depth of Melville's story, of the rewards and dangers, the subtle ins and outs of the quest, one is likely to need a guide, as Ishmael did when he undertook his first whaling voyage in the company of Queequeg. This book is intended as such a guide.

Originally written as a long chapter in a larger study of Melville's major fiction, *The Weaver-God He Weaves: Melville and the Poetics of the Novel* (1996), this essay took the form, almost from the beginning, of a chapter-by-chapter account of my own close encounter with *Moby-Dick*. And as it grew, I realized I was writing a book within a book that might prove useful in its own right to readers of Melville's most difficult and perplexing narrative. So far as I know, there is nothing quite like it, no scene-by-scene discussion, anywhere among the shelves of books devoted to this extraordinary novel. Happily, the editors at the Kent State University Press, publishers of *The Weaver-God,* agreed to the idea of issuing this chapter as a separate volume. The only change in the present volume is a change in title, from "Sounding the Self" to *Sounding the Whale,* a modification that permits the essay to stand more squarely on its own and perhaps more clearly points to the organizing idea in Melville's narrative, namely, that the Whale is Melville's great symbol for the self, his ingenious image of the soul—the object, as his Transcendentalist contemporaries should have recognized, of all meditation.

"To sound" has many meanings, but among the many that are relevant in such an endlessly layered book as *Moby-Dick,* the most important are *to celebrate or honor,* as Ishmael celebrates the Whale and the "honor and glory" of whaling; and *to measure, to investigate or examine, to try to find out,* as Ishmael endlessly measures and investigates the Whale's anatomy, probing it in part and in whole, throughout the notorious cetology chapters especially, to make it yield its wealth of meanings. The whole process, we shall see, is coincident with Ishmael's effort to discover his own buried self or soul, to know its treasure house of qualities, natural and supernatural, and to unleash its immense power within himself.

To be sure, no guide goes alone. I have had my own helping spirits in threading my way through the intricacies of Melville's narrative, most especially C. G. Jung, Joseph Campbell, Northrop Frye, Mircea Eliade, and T. S. Eliot. These seminal thinkers, with their powerful psychological and mythic sensibilities, have helped me to see Melville's subject as one of spiritual discovery, of awakening to self-knowledge. Others, such as Lascelles Abercrombie, Albert Cook, and John Kevin Newman, not to mention the great epic practitioners themselves, Homer, Dante, and Milton, have helped me to see it in the context of Melville's predecessors in this most challenging and profound of literary genres.

My approach, ultimately, is based on a theory of genres, and the assumption that no author, no matter how original, creates in a vacuum. Indeed, rather than view genres and narrative conventions as rule-bound schemes that inhibit creativity, I see them, as Tzvetan Todorov, E. D. Hirsch, Hans Robert Jauss, Jonathan Culler, Robert Scholes, Adena Rosmarin, and others have been teaching us to do in recent years, as *enabling* or making possible the creative process. Generic codes ought not to be regarded simply as classificatory schemes or rule-bound formulae but as communicative codes that make meaning possible and intention discernible. Melville's critics have long assumed that the author of *Moby-Dick* was a raw genius who read widely and energetically but lacked patience for, and even knowledge of, traditional forms of narrative. In the following pages I argue that Melville was well versed in such forms and appropriated them to his own highly original purposes, indeed, that in this novel he set out to fuse the heroic qualities of the ancient Homeric epic with the spiritual qualities of the early modern form found in Dante and Milton, all in an unprecedented poetic prose—the first such prose epic of its kind, and the only religious epic on the subject of whaling anyone has ever had the audacity to write.

Among the many people who contributed to the production of this study, going back even to my undergraduate days, I wish to thank especially a luminous professor, Robert Diebold, then of Carleton College; an astute mentor and critic, Terence Martin, of Indiana University; and a most generous and perceptive colleague and friend, James Maddox, of George Washington University, for their inspiration, faith, and counsel. Even before these three, however, there were my venturesome siblings, John and Steph, who led the way—to school, to the water, and beyond. This book is dedicated to them.

Sounding the Whale: *Moby-Dick* as Epic Novel

At the end of his now famous review, written in the late summer of 1850 while composing *Moby-Dick,* Melville predicted that Hawthorne's *Mosses from an Old Manse* would one day be regarded as his masterpiece. "For," he explained, "there is a sure, though a secret sign in some works which prove the culmination of the powers (only the developable ones, however) that produced them." Whether Melville had read any of Hawthorne's other works at this time is unclear. Still unacquainted with the man himself, or so he professed, he apparently did not know that Hawthorne had published *The Scarlet Letter* earlier that same year.[1] Even so, Melville had the good sense to hedge his bets by adding that he hoped the older writer would yet prove his prediction wrong, "Especially," he explained, "as I somehow cling to the strange fancy, that, in all men, hiddenly reside certain wondrous, occult properties—as in some plants and minerals—which by some happy but very rare accident (as bronze was discovered by the melting of the iron and brass in the burning of Corinth) may chance to be called forth here on earth; not entirely waiting for their better discovery in the more congenial, blessed atmosphere of heaven."[2]

What is remarkable about this rather droll version of Emersonian philosophy is that it captures the same conviction regarding the potency of transcendent powers, the same conception of life, even the same theory of art that Melville was then trying to infuse into his own masterwork. The calling forth of wondrous, occult properties, that rare but happy accident in the life of humankind, is the central subject of Melville's great story. In its most heightened form, it is also the subject of the world's great modern epics, particularly spiritual epics, such as the *Divine Comedy* and *Paradise Lost,* that tell the story of a hero who makes a life-transforming journey into the deepest realms of the self and back out again.

Since 1950, when Newton Arvin and Henry F. Pommer first examined the matter in some detail, many critics have gone on record as calling *Moby-Dick* an epic or acknowledging it has significant ties with the epic tradition.[3] But there have also been many who have questioned such a designation and argued instead for the influence of some other genre, particularly tragedy, romance, or anatomy, or some heterogeneous combination of genres. Even some who advocate reading the book as an epic, such as Arvin or, more recently, John P. McWilliams, have expressed reservations about the term or claimed the book finally eludes generic classification. Clearly, Melville's critics are far from agreement on the matter, despite the fact that it is one of the most analyzed texts in all of American literature. Even among critics who are predisposed to see the book as an epic, there is some disagreement about the qualities that make it so.

While there are several reasons for such disagreement, much of it, I would say, stems from the fact that even as an epic *Moby-Dick* is an unusually ambitious work that brings together two epic traditions rather than one: the ancient or primitive national epic of combat or conflict, as in the *Iliad* or *Beowulf*, and the modern universal epic of spiritual quest, of the search for a transcendent order or significance to human life, as in the *Divine Comedy* or *Paradise Lost*. Though in Melville's treatment the two are in fact woven together to form a single story, with each of the two major characters crossing the line into the other's epic territory, the first can be said to focus generally on Ahab and the second on Ishmael.

While much of my discussion centers on Ahab and the ancient epic of combat, my principal point of focus throughout is on *Moby-Dick* as a spiritual epic. The later tradition envelopes the earlier one, as Ishmael's story envelopes Ahab's. As more and more critics in the twentieth century have testified, this is Ishmael's story even more than it is Ahab's, important as Ahab's is, and so the parallels with the spiritual epic are more pervasive, and more profound, than the parallels with the primitive epic of physical courage. Moreover, given Melville's symbolic technique, which in an epic work is designed to infuse the quotidian world with significance and elevate mundane matters to the supernatural plane, the theme of the quest for the soul takes on an overriding importance. The ancient epics, too, of course had a spiritual dimension in that they were intended to explain the intrusions of the gods into the affairs of humankind; they were, as Arthur Hutson and Patricia McCoy, among others, have said, concerned in a fundamental way with mythology.[4] But, beginning with Dante, the epic became essentially inward, and not simply psychological but spiritual, centering on the search for the soul or the soul's salvation. As an epic of the universal story of mankind, therefore, *Moby-Dick* is more than a local instance of mythmaking or nation-building, comparable for its time and place to the *Odyssey* of ancient Greece or the *Aeneid* of early Rome. It is also Melville's attempt to show that the powers behind the great spiritual epics of the world are the same powers that propelled its major religious mythologies—Judeo-Christian, Hindu, Egyptian, among others Melville knew quite thoroughly[5]—and that they were as alive in his own day as they had been in those earlier times.[6]

My understanding of Melville's conception of epic writing has been much informed by several searching studies of the epic poem, especially work by Lascelles Abercrombie, Albert Cook, and John Kevin Newman.[7] However, my understanding of Melville's conception of the epic journey or quest in particular is even more deeply indebted to the work of several modern students of psychology, religion, and myth, especially C. G. Jung, Mircea Eliade, and Joseph Campbell, who define life, and the quest, in terms of individuation or spiritual awakening and otherwise explore, from a modern, broadly psychological point of view, the gap between the seen and the unseen, the known and the unknown worlds. Campbell offers the classic formulation, in *The Hero with a Thousand Faces,* though he in no way restricts his discussion to the epic per se, when he says that the hero's journey is structured like the "monomyth" found in rites of passage, with their three-part structure of separation, initiation or trial, and return. As Campbell says, "A hero ventures forth from the world of common day into a region of supernatural wonder: fabulous forces are there encountered and a decisive victory is won: the hero comes back from this mysterious adventure with the power to bestow boons on his fellow man."[8] The Greek legends of Prometheus and Jason, the biblical narratives of Moses and Christ, the legend of the Buddha, and the epic stories of Odysseus and Aeneas all follow this basic pattern, typically represented in terms of the hero's being swallowed by a monster and then being reborn.

When seen in relation to *Moby-Dick,* such a scheme, with its emphasis on transformation and the turning toward spiritual self-knowledge, naturally points to Ishmael as the true hero of the book; he alone completes an initiatory test and returns to tell about it, though the nature of his "boon" may at first seem problematic. By contrast, Ahab resists the test, even as he resists all reminders of his mortality. In Eliade's terms, he clings to his existence as a "natural" man and is never "born to the spirit."[9] As is often the case, however, there are larger social and political consequences to such resistance. Entrusted with the power to rule others, Ahab is an instance of the public man turned private person. Like the king who becomes a tyrant, a dangerous figure known in myth and folklore as "Holdfast," he sacrifices the public good for his own benefit.[10] Unredeemed and unreborn, Ahab is incapable of recognizing anything beyond his own egoistic needs, and as a consequence he brings not health nor treasure nor sacred knowledge but ruin and death to his people and to himself.

In the following discussion, I have taken a cue from Ishmael, a model anatomist, and dissected *Moby-Dick* into pieces, in this case five sections of nearly equal length. I have done so for practical reasons and as a convenience to the reader, who would no doubt otherwise find this an impossibly long discussion. But I have done so also to call attention to a five-part structure that I believe is inherent to the narrative itself. This structure takes its definition from the stages in the whale hunt that forms the basic story line of the book: (1) preparations for the hunt (chapters 1–23); (2) presentation of the lore of the whaling industry (chapters 24–47); (3) the pursuit of the whale (chapters 48–76); (4) capturing the whale (chapters 77–105); and (5) the trial in the whale's "belly" (chapters 106–35). For each of these parts, I have appropriated a corresponding section title from T. S. Eliot's *The Waste Land* to indicate in a shorthand form how Melville unfolds the central themes of the hunt for the great White Whale. Both works, in fact, the one for the nineteenth century and the other for the twentieth, make extensive use of many of the same central images, of death and burial, of games and the hunt, of fire and water, of lightning, thunder, and rain. More importantly, both are epic works that tell much the same story of a devastated land, a wounded fisher king, and the search for a holy elixir or precious fluid, whether of whale oil or water.[11]

The first clues that *Moby-Dick* belongs with the world's great epics are to be found in the etymology and extracts sections of the book's frontmatter. Here, Melville creates the impression that his subject is universal and that, like the old oral epics, his story is a work of bricolage. To appropriate a distinction first made by Lascelles Abercrombie, one of the pioneering students of the form, the extracts are the epic material—"fragmentary, scattered, loosely related, sometimes contradictory"—out of which Melville's epic poetry was made.[12] Even before the current storyteller, in this case Ishmael, had come along to put together the pieces, there had been earlier bards, in sundry cultures and languages, who sang of his subject. By implication, the whale is everywhere and immortal. The etymologies and extracts help to establish the epic stature, formidableness, and inexhaustibility of Ishmael's subject, and they serve to place the reader in an appropriate mood of awe or wonder.

Yet they also help to establish the character of Melville's storyteller, even before he introduces himself. They suggest the compiler himself to be a broken, searching, strangely modern figure, sometimes a lexicographer, sometimes a sub-sub-librarian, and at other times an author or a whaler, whose world is fragmented almost beyond repair—a man so preoccupied with the beast of destruction as to be at once possessed and at the same time paralyzed. Like Tiresias, the narrator of Eliot's poem, he is all but overwhelmed by the oppressiveness of death and destruction, trapped in a past without change, and can therefore do little more than murmur, "These fragments I have shored against my ruins."[13] Together, the extracts reveal the compiler's fixation on Leviathan, the ancient initiator of the Last Things, at the same time they reveal his numbness, or shock, and his inability to make sense of what he has lived through.

But the opening extracts have a redemptive function as well.[14] Like the scattered pieces of a fertility god, they await the water that will restore life to the dead land, and its people, in some distant spring. In effect, they are like seeds of the hero's renewal, as the writings of the past often are. But their mystery first must be unlocked; a worthy hero who can show the way must make himself known. Even before the story begins, then, Melville hints at important parallels between his story of the wounded Ahab, named for a despised Old Testament king, and the ancient myth of the impotent Fisher King, whose land has been devastated by his own selfishness and who now awaits a cure.

One final word of introduction: As almost anyone who has ever looked closely into Melville's novel knows, *Moby-Dick* is an incredibly rich and complex work with as intricate a set of symbols, image patterns, and motifs as is to be found in a work of literature anywhere in the world. One of the things I hope to show in the succeeding pages is that there is a logic to Melville's patterning, a logic driven by his understanding of and excitement for the epic genre but given form by a language of nature that is universal—of decay and rebirth, of seasonal cycles, of water, fire, thunder, lightning. I cannot, of course, say whether Melville himself was fully conscious of the intricate web of relations I trace in this chapter. But I believe that, as he himself said in his review of Hawthorne's *Mosses,* there is something "wondrous" or "occult" about certain instances of the creative process that make them transcend what can normally be expected in such matters. Certainly to those of us who have never written an epic, particularly one of such depth and grandeur and richness as *Moby-Dick,* there is something preternatural about the form itself. Perhaps it is true, too, that there is something preternatural also about the effort required to produce one.

I. THE BURIAL OF THE DEAD

Like the *Divine Comedy, The Waste Land,* and other spiritual epics, *Moby-Dick* opens with its hero in a fallen state of emotional torpor and confusion. Starting his story before his transforming experience on the *Pequod,* Ishmael says he is like a spiritually dead man in a spiritually dead land, seeking the relief of the condemned everywhere. He has grown weary of existence, as one does when his youth is spent and he finds himself, as Dante said at the start of his story, "In the middle of the journey of our life." He experiences depression, morbidness, even thoughts of suicide, and he hungers for change or escape.

Like Ahab, Ishmael suffers from a malaise or schism in the soul, an aggression so intense as to prove deadly to himself and others. As Ishmael confesses, it is only by holding to "a strong moral principle" that he can keep himself from "deliberately stepping into the street, and methodically knocking people's hats off." Whenever he finds himself overtaken by such an urge, he knows it is "high time to get to sea as soon as I can." However, whether this is to be viewed as a still surer means of realizing a deep-seated death wish or as an alternative to it, a means of regaining his health, Ishmael himself seems a little unsure. Going to sea, he says equivocally, "is my substitute for pistol and ball."[15] Even if he himself is unsure, his unconscious knows there must be a dying to the world before there can be a rebirth. That is the only way one can ever hope to overcome the death of the spirit. Ahab's example attests to that by his failure, as Ishmael's example does by his success. For the hero to come back as one reborn, filled with creative energy, as Ishmael does when he returns to tell his tale at the end, he must first give up the world and everything in it.

It is significant, but not widely recognized, that Ishmael is not alone in his suffering, that he is a representative figure or exemplary hero. "If they but knew it," he writes, "almost all men in their degree, some time or other, cherish very nearly the same feelings towards the ocean with me," and as proof he has to look no further than his own fellow "Manhattoes." Everywhere he looks, on a dreamy Sunday afternoon, he sees "crowds of water-gazers," thirsting for the adventure that will free them from the land and the deadly routine of their lives. All of them, "thousands upon thousands of mortal men fixed in ocean reveries," hunger for that deeper, vivifying knowledge of the spirit that going to sea makes possible. "Meditation and water," Ishmael explains, "are wedded forever" because, as the Greeks were the first to learn, introspection is the way to self-understanding (3–4). However, as the example of Narcissus warns, such inwardness can be a dangerous business; it must not lead simply to a love for the self or a fascinated preoccupation. It has to be conducted as an active search for and testing of the self; it has to involve a trial. Few people get beyond the stage of being weekend water-gazers because they are afraid of the challenge of the new, afraid of what the unfamiliar might hold. They thus remain among the dead, "victims" whom one day a more adventurous soul, like Ishmael, will come back to try to rescue, and so on, in an endless cycle.

What distinguishes Ishmael from these more timid Manhattanites is simply that he accepts the call to the sea. He does so, to be sure, without full understanding of what he is doing or why, but he is the sort of man who lives intuitively and knows to trust his inner promptings wherever they might lead him. Because the episodes in his journey represent trials of the spirit, psychological trials, his passage is inward as much as it is across land or water—"into depths where obscure resistances are overcome," as Campbell explains, "and long lost, forgotten powers are revivified, to be made available for the transfiguration of the world."[16]

In *Moby-Dick* this inner realm is of course represented by the sea, a universal image of the unconscious, where all the monsters and helping figures of childhood are to be found, along with the many talents and other powers that lie dormant within every adult. Chief among these, in Ishmael's case, is the complicated image of the Whale itself, which is all these things and more and also serves as the "herald" that calls him to his adventure. At the end of chapter 1, "Loomings," with its promise of some distant, portentous engagement, Ishmael reveals that his chief motive for wanting to go whaling "was the overwhelming idea of the great whale himself." But that he is responding as much to a lure from within the self as from without is suggested in the final lines of this opening chapter, when he asserts that, having examined his motives and finding the idea of going whaling to his liking, "the great flood-gates of the wonder-world swung open, and in the wild conceits that swayed me to my purpose, two and two there floated in my inmost soul, endless processions of the whale, and, midmost of them all, one grand hooded phantom, like a snow hill in the air" (7). For Melville's hero, this phantom whale that is later incarnated as the great White Whale is the beginning and the end, and it represents all the instinctual vitality locked deep within the self. It is in this sense that the Whale is synonymous with "the ungraspable phantom of life" that is "the key to it all" (5).

Because the way of the hero is through a strange realm filled with danger and hardship, he requires the help of a guide or wisdom figure, some master of the world beyond who can provide the kind of assistance that, to the neophyte, seems magical. As in any initiatory experience, the novice has to be instructed in the rules of the game and have the way pointed out to him. Also, usually the guide supplies a charm or fetish that will serve to ward off danger or insulate the hero from the dark forces unleashed during this process. While the guide is sometimes a woman, like Beatrice in Dante's vision, more typically it is a man, as in the *Divine Comedy* again, where Virgil assumes the role in the early stages. So in *Moby-Dick* Ishmael is guided through the early episodes of his journey by the masterful harpooner and mystagogue, Queequeg, a deeply if comically religious man whose home is a mythical island called Kokovoko. In keeping with such mysterious figures generally, Queequeg is both protective and forbidding, nurturing and threatening, like the complex powers of the unconscious that he symbolizes.[17]

When Ishmael meets Queequeg, on his first night at the Spouter-Inn, while en route to his initial whaling adventure, the unlettered cannibal seems a most unlikely candidate for a mentor in any regard, except possibly the art of embalming. Queequeg, who has been out late peddling shrunken heads in the streets of New Bedford, looks like something out of a nightmare (Ishmael, it will be noted, had been struggling to fall asleep when the savage makes his entrance into his room), with strange tattoos all over his body, a hideous scalp-knot on his head, and a frightful tomahawk at his side. Ishmael, who admits to being "as much afraid of him as if it was the devil himself" when he first glimpses him, is initially horror-struck that he might lose his own head to this "abominable savage" (22). As it turns out, of course, Queequeg is not a cannibal; but, in the logic of the book, his reputation as a man-eater does make him an appropriate guide for a novice like Ishmael, whose initiation will require that he be swallowed by a Whale. Though Ishmael "ain't insured!" as he exclaims in desperation to the landlord, he could hardly do better than to trust himself to this implausible guide who will one day save him from the wrath of the great White Whale. Even on this first night, after all the proper introductions have been made, he comes somehow to sense that this peculiar figure is a kind of blessing in disguise, so much so that, after dismissing Peter Coffin, he turned in, as he says, "and never slept better in my life" (24). Having once before that evening gone to bed commending himself "to the care of heaven" (20), he can do so now with a true sense of security. To the hero who can bring himself to believe in the ultimate benevolence of the creation, all the security of an assisting providence will be given.

Still, if Ishmael knew how to read the signs, he would know his destiny had brought him to the one man who can lead him through the maze of his future trials and on to the final, life-changing encounter with the beast of destruction. The next morning, waking to find Queequeg's arm thrown over him in a loving, protective embrace, he sees only that "this arm of his [was] tattooed all over with an interminable Cretan labyrinth of a figure" (25). Ishmael is too green at this point to recognize that this figure represents a map of the path in and out of the maze of the Minotaur, the beast he must slay to gain whatever treasure awaits him. He can hardly be expected to know, at this early stage of the hunt, that he himself will become an American version of Theseus. However, much later in the narrative, in "A Bower in the Arsacides" (chapter 102), he will turn up with a tattoo on his own right arm bearing the dimensions of a gigantic whale, whose labyrinthine skeleton he has wandered into and out of again. An experienced whaler himself by this time, Ishmael is then ready to lead his readers into the belly of the whale and out again. In the end, he becomes their guide and protector, the hero who shows the way.

The next morning, though, when Ishmael ventures into the streets of New Bedford, he is startled to find himself in the midst of an entire society completely devoted to the business of whaling. Virtually all the males of the town are living at a stage much in advance of the Manhattanites who manage to get only as far as the water's edge in their longing to go to sea. As Ishmael goes out to survey the local scene, he is astonished to discover the streets are full of seasoned whalers just like Queequeg, not simply "the queerest looking nondescripts from foreign parts," but "savages outright"—Feegeeans, Tongatabooans, Erromanggoans—as well as "scores of green Vermonters and New Hampshire men, all athirst for gain and glory in the fishery" (31). The whole town, the entire industry, it seems, is set up to initiate young men into the ways of the hunt.

But such appearances are deceptive. The rites of passage of New England farmboys are only incidental to the basic mission of America's foremost whaling town, namely, the accumulation of huge fortunes. "Nowhere in all America," Ishmael writes, "will you find more patrician-like houses; parks and gardens more opulent, than in New Bedford." A virtual "land of oil," the "town itself is perhaps the dearest place to live in, in all New England," its wealth all "harpooned and dragged up hither from the bottom of the sea" (32). The whole town, in other words, is dedicated to acquiring only the lowest form of treasure that whaling can bring. Fortunately, Ishmael, who only the night before had escaped the ashy, Gomorrah-like inn called "The Trap," somehow knows not to undertake the hunt for material gain only. Intuitively, he recognizes he must push on to Nantucket, the one place in the world where the simple values of the original whale hunters are still practiced, and embark from there.

Melville spells out the dangers of the hero's quest, particularly the dangers of his seeking only earthly profits, in "The Chapel." Here Ishmael, still a relatively conventional hero seeking a conventional form of strength in a conventional place, becomes one of "a small scattered congregation of sailors, and sailors' wives and widows" who sit in silence contemplating the burial of the dead at sea. On his way to the chapel, he had experienced a sudden change in the weather, from "sunny cold" to "driving sleet and mist," a change that emblematizes the changeability of the earthly realm that is the theme of this chapter (34). Once inside, Ishmael sits with the others staring at a series of marble tablets, which flank the pulpit, bearing the names and other details of the lives of sailors lost at sea—stark reminders of the mutability of human existence and human fortune. Although later, when he signs on the *Pequod,* Ishmael shows a healthy regard for the advantages of earning a good wage, in this scene he comes to recognize that to be paid can never be the chief object of the hunt. For he discovers his own mortality and witnesses the folly of a life dedicated to heaping up material riches. In the chapel, he sees that one must choose between death as an ultimate end and faith in some afterlife or spiritual principle. But he also sees that, for a thinking man like himself, the choice is always tenuous and that true faith is never free of entanglements with the world. As he says, in an odd, haunting image, "Faith, like a jackal, feeds among the tombs, and even from these dead doubts she gathers her most vital hope" (37). Still, the need to conquer death, or look beyond it, to seek the soul and live out of it, is at last clear. This is the true reason for undertaking the hunt for the whale, and in the chapel scene this becomes Ishmael's overriding motive.

Although initially sobered by the many memento mori in the chapel, Ishmael somehow manages to grow "merry" again and jokes that he can even consider a stove boat as a "fine chance for promotion" to a higher realm. "Methinks we have hugely mistaken this matter of Life and Death," he exclaims. "Methinks that what they call my shadow here on earth is my true substance. . . . Methinks my body is but the lees of my better being. In fact," he says, unconsciously contrasting himself with his future captain, Ahab, who regards every limb as sacred, "take my body who will, take it I say, it is not me. And therefore three cheers for Nantucket; and come a stove boat and stove body when they will, for stave my soul, Jove himself cannot" (37). Despite the obvious bravado of this outburst, Ishmael here makes it clear that he has survived his first test and will emerge from this curious Chapel Perilous a profoundly changed man.

Before looking at the sermon that serves as a gloss on this all-important first step in Ishmael's transformation, it is necessary to look briefly at Father Mapple, the complex, sometimes baffling chaplain who delivers it. A man of God, and agent of the Father (as his Catholic-sounding nickname rather obviously implies), he too had gone to sea in his youth and served as a harpooner in the whaling industry. Old in years and experience, then, yet forever young in appearance, he is thus a fit guide for young petitioners. But unlike Queequeg, Mapple counsels caution and obedience. He is in fact an example of a special kind of guide, called in Jung's term a "threshold guardian," who stands at the gateway to the realm of supernatural power and warns the tender or fainthearted to stay away. Conservative and cautious by nature, like the parents of young children, such a figure purposely tries to delimit the hero's world on every side, in accordance with the abilities of the aspirant. When Mapple speaks, therefore, he is like the ancient oracles who guarded the path of the supplicant; he warns the would-be adventurer to stay within the confines of the known world and to flee all fearful encounters with the great powers beyond. To be sure, as a threshold guardian, it is not Mapple's job to frighten away *all* comers; on the contrary, his function is to make sure that the few who finally do come forward are truly ready to take the plunge, that they have the courage and skill to survive the challenges of the next stage of the journey.

After Father Mapple climbs up to his pulpit, he stands to deliver his sermon from behind a copy of the Bible. Immediately sizing him up, Ishmael senses that what he is about to speak is the truth, not because it conforms to the standard Judaeo-Christian view, but because what the chaplain brings to his congregation is the water of renewal. Mapple himself speaks from the very midst of it. "[R]eplenished with the meat and wine of the word," Ishmael explains, "to the faithful man of God, this pulpit, I see, is a self-containing stronghold—a lofty Ehrenbreitstein, with a perennial well of water within the walls" (39). Mapple's sermon, however, is deceptive, as dual-edged as the man himself. What he preaches is indeed a "two-stranded lesson" (42). While on the one hand he speaks to the many whose hearts are not yet ready, preaching against sin and disobedience, and counseling repentance and submission to the will of God; on the other, he also speaks to the few, like Ishmael, who may at that very moment be on the threshold of the potentially deadly yet also potentially glorious adventure of the hero.

Properly understood, the story of Jonah, though couched in the familiar biblical language of sin and trial and deliverance, is a universal tale of one who actively refuses the call to the soul's awakening. It thus serves as a warning, and an invitation, to those who might be resisting or wavering on the brink. What Mapple says is paradoxical: the call is irresistible; the call must be freely accepted. Clearly there is no escaping the experience of being trapped in the belly of the whale, if that is one's destiny. Whether one refuses, like Jonah, or accepts the call, as Ishmael does, there is no avoiding the experience of death and burial, of suffering and dismemberment, when it finally comes.[18] There is only the hope of surviving it in some new form, the hope of some ultimate redemption or miraculous return from the dead, as Jonah returns in the end.

In Melville's conception, the call to adventure, the call to spiritual awakening, was equivalent to the Puritan experience of grace; and, to the rational mind, it entailed the same contradictory dynamic of fate and free will. Like his Calvinist forebears, Melville understood the call as an invitation to experience the woe and delight of the loss of ego that leads to the discovery of the self or the soul, one's core identity. Though one of the smallest books in the Scriptures, Mapple exclaims of Jonah's story, while underscoring the sermon's true theme, "what depths of the soul does Jonah's deep sea-line sound!" (42). The chaplain's rendering of Jonah's tale constitutes a paradigm of the central situation of Melville's epic as a whole, of the trials of the self and its transformation, its breakup and recovery in the belly of the beast. As such, it deserves careful scrutiny.

In Mapple's rendering, the story of Jonah is the story of a man bent on escaping his identity, the identity of his destiny. Jonah's every move, every encounter, reveals this to be so. As he steps onto the ship bound for Tarshish, all the sailors stop to stare at him and wonder *who he is*. And almost immediately, as if in answer to their question, someone calls him a "parricide," a seemingly offhand remark that, ironically, provides an important clue to his identity (43). For in refusing the call to do his Father's bidding, Jonah in effect "kills the father" in himself, the source of spiritual life, of empowering identity, at his center. He refuses to grow up. When the Captain, hearing Jonah coming toward his cabin, calls out "Who's there?" the innocent request to identify himself "mangles" Jonah, an early sign that, for Melville, Jonah's story is linked with Ahab's, as well as Ishmael's, and that the process of dismemberment is symbolic of the pain of personal transformation (44).

It is only when the "hard hand of God" presses on Jonah, forcing him to answer the crew's demands to reveal who he is, that the object of his trial is defined as nothing more or less than the acceptance of his identity. It is only when he begins to confess who he is—first tentatively, "I am a Hebrew," he cries at the height of the storm, thus identifying himself as one of the chosen; then more emphatically, "I fear the Lord the God of Heaven"—that the process of recovering his true self can begin in earnest. For it is then that his shipmates throw him into the sea, where he is carried down "into the yawning jaws awaiting him" (46). There, having owned up to his earthly identity as "one who fears the Lord," he finally accepts God's call, repents his waywardness, and discovers his spiritual identity as one who is delivered by the Lord. In Hebrew Jonah means "dove." And as we know from the story of Noah and elsewhere, the dove carries the sign of peace; it brings news of deliverance from death.

Mapple's sermon does more than warn against refusing the call, however. It also defines the marks of those who do and those who do not refuse it, and as such it provides a means for judging Ishmael's motives, his readiness to undertake the journey, and for determining why Ahab's quest is destined to fail. First of all, until the adventurer owns who he is and recognizes the need to make the journey he is called to, he lives as a man who is already dead, as Jonah does when he "sleeps" with a "dead ear" in his tomblike berth below the ship's waterline (45). That is to say, he feels trapped in his own ego. Secondly, he must "pay" for his own passage. As Mapple says, in this world it is "sin that pays its way" (44). Like Ahab, who in the end pays for his passage on the *Pequod* with the gold doubloon, the "God-fugitive" Jonah is willing to pay much more than the standard fare if that will permit him to escape his destiny (46). But of course those who refuse the call cannot escape having to pay spiritually, too, for their waywardness. That is why they die. Without an infinite source of vitality to sustain them, without a soul, their lives eventually run out.

As it is for Jonah, so it is for these others; the guilty conscience of the resisting hero "is a wound, and there's naught to staunch it" (45). His spiritual lifeblood would all eventually leak away, leaving him dead. Only if it were replenished endlessly, as it would be if he possessed the oil of the whale, would the lamp of his soul burn eternally.[19] In sum, the marks of those who refuse the call, who remain imprisoned by their earthly identity, are these: a feeling of spiritual deadness and entrapment; a sense of life's meagerness, and apprehension at its eventually running out; a desperate desire to hold on, to pay any price but the one required of them; a great fear of God and of not being chosen; and the profound dread that there will be no boon or prize at the end of the game.[20]

In the end, after being reborn "out of the belly of hell," when Jonah is commanded a second time, he answers the call to do "the Almighty's bidding." He agrees to do his duty by preaching "the Truth to the Face of Falsehood"; he goes to Nineveh and brings the prophecy of the deliverance from death of the people there (47–48). Following his own deliverance, Jonah thus becomes an instance of the returning hero, an image of the many figures in *Moby-Dick* who speak as prophets to the dead—of Father Mapple, Elijah, Pip, and finally Ishmael. Melville, however, shows us little of the returning Jonah. Instead, it is Father Mapple who fills out the image of the returning hero in his role as boon-carrier.[21] Significantly, he is a man of the word, an artist, a truth-teller, like Melville himself. When he speaks, the signs are on him that God speaks through him; the "light" that leaps from his eye, the "thunders" that roll away from his brow, these make his listeners look on him with the sense they are looking on the Godhead itself, "with a quick fear that was strange to them" (47).

Yet even Mapple is a reluctant hero; what he shows by his example is how difficult it is to return to the human fold after the intense inwardness and sublimity of the hunt. As he explains to his congregation, "[while] God has laid but one hand upon you; both his hands press upon me." The boon becomes a terrible burden; to be a "speaker of true things," to sound "unwelcome truths in the ears of a wicked Nineveh," to speak to the dead of their deadness and suffer the enmity of the damned is a hard thing.

Fortunately, there is a power to sustain the returning quester—the power of God, of the deepest self. In an image that defines the central meaning of Melville's great symbol of the Whale, there is the power of Leviathan itself, its breeching a trope for the birth of the soul out of the depths of its imprisonment, as it is in Mapple's sermon. Instantaneously, when Jonah finally speaks his own name, when he cries out his identity for the first time, "Then God spake unto the fish [that confined him]; and from the shuddering cold and blackness of the sea, the whale came breeching up towards the warm and pleasant sun, and all the delights of air and earth" (47–48). As this image powerfully suggests, the birth of the self is an occurrence of incredible force, and of transcendent beauty and joy. Though there is a burden to the hero's return, a "woe," it is more than compensated by the "delight" he experiences in performing his true calling. At the culminating moment, when Mapple begins his peroration on the theme of "delight," the chaplain speaks the overriding thesis of his sermon, and of the whole first section of *Moby-Dick,* when he exclaims, "Delight is to him,—a far, far upward, and inward delight—who against the proud gods and commodores of this earth, ever stands forth his own inexorable self" (48).

Chapter 10, "A Bosom Friend," the first of several in the portrait of Queequeg, presents another imposing, yet this time also comic, example of a character who knows how to stand forth "his own inexorable self." Like the New Bedford chaplain, Queequeg is at one with his god and seems to command all the powers of the earth. Where Mapple moves easily through the driving rain (the water that restores or destroys) on his way to the Whalemen's Chapel, Queequeg sits comfortably before the hearth fire (the fire that revives or kills) in the Spouter-Inn. Where Mapple refashions the word of God to suit his ministerial purpose, Queequeg reworks the countenance of his little surrogate god, Yojo, to suit his inner vision. Neither man's action is sacrilegious because both work out of the inner necessity of the returning hero. Both have seen the face of the Father, and now, each in his independent way, they have come back to the fold to relate what they have witnessed, and to do the work they are bidden to do.

Yet as the title of this chapter suggests, Queequeg is more than the guide who will show Ishmael the way to the hidden god. He *is* the god, an image of that "inexorable self" at the center of every successful hero. A pagan, savage and illiterate, he had a "hideously marred" face with "something in it," Ishmael says vaguely, "which was by no means disagreeable." Yet what that something is he then proceeds to identify, with deadpan irony, when he exclaims, "You cannot hide the soul" (49). Though on the way to Nantucket a greenhorn mistakes Queequeg for "the devil," Ishmael has already gone far enough in his initiation to be able to see in the Polynesian's deep, dark eyes "tokens of a spirit that would dare a thousand devils" (60, 50). If he "looked like a man who had never cringed and never had had a creditor," as Ishmael observes of him, no doubt it is because he never had a cause to fear anything and never had a need to borrow. Wholly centered in himself, he has "no desire to enlarge his circle of acquaintances"; but when his friends come to him, as Ishmael does, he is happy to reciprocate, and more (50). Possessing more of the world's wealth than he himself will ever need, he gives half his thirty pieces of silver, and more, to his new friend, Ishmael. In his own example, he thus makes clear that the world will always provide the initiate whatever he needs to make his journey. To the poor hero like Ishmael, who has the courage to make the first step, life becomes a veritable cornucopia, supplying both bed and counterpane, an evening of good talk, a long smoke, and a friend who "would gladly die for me, if need should be" (51). If he also has to be forced to take an embalmed head into the bargain, that is because, unlike Queequeg, he still has no more desire to be reminded of his mortality than any other poor mortal.

Still, more important than these outward signs of the warming of the world, in the midst of New Bedford's arctic winter, are the signs of warming taking place within Ishmael himself, now that he has made friends with Queequeg. Sitting in their room, the "fire burning low," watching the cannibal count the pages of a "marvelous book" (presumably the Bible), he suddenly became "sensible of strange feelings. I felt a melting in me. No more my splintered heart and maddened hand were turned against the wolfish world. This soothing savage had redeemed it" (50–51).

Later, after the two have formally declared their friendship, Ishmael shows the powerful effect of his transformation when, unlike Jonah before him, he jumps at the chance to do the Lord's bidding. In a comic scene, Ishmael shows he is, if anything, a little too quick to preach his own religion, his "particular Presbyterian form of worship," to a real pagan. For, the way he sees it, he has to "turn idolator" and become a pagan himself first if he is to have any influence with Queequeg (52). Still, as the result of his efforts, Ishmael goes to bed not alone, as Jonah did, but with a friend; not with a conscience wracked by guilt, as Jonah had, but with one "at peace"; not to sleep like a dead man but to lie abed "chatting and napping" at intervals and then to awake refreshed long before daybreak (53). There, in the cold and the dark, after the fire has gone out, Ishmael speaks for the first time not simply of feeling his "identity" but of feeling it "aright," as if "darkness were indeed the proper element of our essences," he theorizes, "though light be more congenial to our clayey part" (54). Now, warmed by an interior fire, Ishmael has no need for any other kind of flame.

The next day, as the two of them glide down the Acushnet River on the way out of town toward Nantucket, they see ice-crusted New Bedford off to one side, "huge hills and mountains of casks on casks piled upon her wharves" (60). These casks are of course intended to hold the precious whale oil that is the town's principal source of wealth. However, they are really more like stacks of coffins, or caskets, that lie there mutely waiting to serve the burial of the dead instead. To the mind prepared to look for the "meaning" of things, as Ishmael does with comic self-consciousness in the New Bedford chapters, and acknowledge the pervasiveness of death in this wintry landscape, they serve as reminders that America's most affluent town is, after all, a land of the dead and must be abandoned.

By contrast, Nantucket seems impoverished and unpromising. To the worldly eye, it is a wasteland, a desert of sand—"all beach, without a background." But despite the barrenness of the landscape, the people of Nantucket enjoy a wealth and power that those of New Bedford and other whaling centers can hardly appreciate. For like "sea hermits, issuing from their ant-hill in the sea," these "naked Nantucketers" have "overrun and conquered the watery world like so many Alexanders; parcelling out among them the Atlantic, Pacific, and Indian oceans, as the three pirate powers did Poland." As is soon evident in Ishmael's dealings with the Quaker Bildad, the Nantucketers can be shrewd, grasping materialists, but they possess a wealth beyond material riches, too. So at home is the Nantucket whaler while at sea, so attuned to its powerful rhythms, that at night, like the landless gull, he "furls his sails, and lays him to his rest, while under his very pillow rush herds of walruses and whales" (63–64). A nation of adventuring heroes, the people of Nantucket command the wealth of all the seas, the wealth of dreams and the unconscious, as this oceanic image of natural power makes clear.

Like most chapter titles in *Moby-Dick,* "Chowder," the title of the next chapter, is a metaphor or conceit. Besides suggesting something of the mixed character of Ishmael's initial experience of Nantucket, it offers a preview, in miniature, of the mixed nature of the whaling life generally. Arriving at the Try-Pots Inn, Ishmael is immediately reminded by the gallows on the sign outside that there is death and damnation in the whaleman's calling. If one is not killed or maimed in the hunt, the despair at failure can be just as devastating and lead to the same result. Mistress Hussey lectures Queequeg about a recent suicide in her apartments, a young man named Stiggs, who, "coming from that unfort'nt v'y'ge of his," as she says, "when he was gone four years and a half, with ony three barrels of *ile,* was found dead in my first floor back, with his harpoon in his side," a would-be Christ but one forsaken by the Father (67).

However, just as there is both clam and cod on the bill of fare at the Try-Pots Inn, so is there both death and life in the business of whaling. The cook in the kitchen will sometimes mix up the order and serve "clam" (symbol of the recalcitrance of life, of the withholding side of the dual-edged female principle): "that's a rather cold and clammy reception in the winter time, ain't it, Mrs. Hussey?" complains Ishmael facetiously, when his dinner order arrives.

But the boldest adventurer will generally get "cod" (symbol of the potency of life, of the providential side of the dual-edged male principle), as Ishmael discovers when he steps to the kitchen window and barks out his order to be sure there will be no mistake about it. "Ask," saith the Lord, according to the well-known proverb, "and ye shall be given." In this world, even the adventuring hero sometimes has to take potluck; but if he is truly fearless about tapping its wealth, he will be rewarded beyond even his wildest dreams. When asked, at the end of this chapter, whether he and Queequeg will take clam or cod the next morning for breakfast, Ishmael responds with the boldness of one who has learned to stand forth his own inexorable self, "Both; and let's have a couple of smoked herring by way of variety," he adds cheekily (67).

"God helps those who help themselves"—that is the unwritten motto of the successful adventurer, and that is the surprising lesson of the following chapter, "The Ship." Though the hero can hardly know such a thing in the beginning, the person who serves as a guide is simply a symbol of the assisting power that dwells within everyone. He is, as in the case of Queequeg, an image of the soul of the adventurer, his task being to instill in his new friend an abiding confidence in his own powers. Thus Ishmael, despite the newfound brazenness displayed at the end of the previous chapter, expresses "surprise and no small concern" when Queequeg informs him that the little god Yojo wants Ishmael himself to be the one to select their ship. Speaking like the novice he is, Ishmael nervously admits that "I did not like that plan at all. I had not a little relied upon Queequeg's sagacity to point out the whaler best fitted to carry us and our fortunes securely." Yet the next morning, his courage screwed up to a pitch, he accomplishes his task quickly and with little worry or internal debate. Ostensibly entrusting everything to the little god Yojo, the comic fetish or charm that seems to protect Ishmael in Queequeg's absence, he in fact falls back on his own intuition in choosing the *Pequod* over the several other ships then in port (67–68). Though in the course of his adventures he sometimes claims to be a victim of the mysterious Fates, it should be recognized that, for the most part, in important ways Ishmael really is the master of his own destiny.

The first part of his day's work successfully completed, Ishmael is nonetheless little wiser than when he began. Boarding the *Pequod* to propose himself as a "candidate" for the voyage, his first response is to look around the quarterdeck "for some one having authority" (70). Clearly, he has not yet figured out that all authority comes from within. Several pages later, though he has by then met with both Captains Peleg and Bildad and taken care of all necessary details, he ends the scene still hungering to see the man who is really in charge. Having only heard about Captain Ahab at this point, Ishmael feels the mystery of his authority deepen. For at this point he learns only that there is much more to know about him. Not until much later are we shown that, behind Ahab, there is a higher authority still, and that Ahab, the son of a "crazy, widowed mother," also seeks the Father (79). Here, however, everything that transpires demonstrates, in an understated way, what Ishmael is not yet prepared to know—namely, that in all essential matters the final authority must reside within the adventurer's own soul.

The encounter with Peleg and Bildad is structured as a second major threshold scene, where Ishmael's resolve and worthiness are tested and he is revealed to be one of the chosen few. Almost literally, in stepping onto the *Pequod,* Ishmael steps into the mouth of the whale, the entrance to the place of trial. For the ship has been rebuilt out of various parts of the whalemen's catch over a long span of years, and the curious wigwam in which he is subjected to Peleg's rigorous questioning is actually supported by the jawbones of a right whale.

Like Father Mapple, Peleg has the job of separating false aspirants from true ones. Those who are not yet ready to follow the path, he tries to dissuade, or intimidate, while those of pure heart and steady purpose he tries to encourage or help smooth their way. Like a holy man conducting an inquest of a heretic, Peleg questions Ishmael about his previous experience at sea. And like a true master, he begins by asking the key question concerning the ultimate test of the whale-hunting hero: "ever been in a stove boat?" Immediately sensing in the politeness of Ishmael's reply ("No, Sir, I never have") that he is a perfect neophyte, Peleg goes back to the beginning and inquires, with the disgust of one who is prepared to hear the worst, "Dost know nothing at all about whaling, I dare say—eh?" When Ishmael confesses his complete ignorance, but then proceeds to mention his previous experience in the merchant service, Peleg cuts him off in disgust and then offers a hint as to the peculiar nature of the whaling enterprise that might help to set him back on track: "Marchant service be damned," he exclaims. "Talk not that lingo to me. Dost see that leg?—I'll take that leg away from thy stern, if ever thou talkest of the marchant service to me again. Marchant service indeed!" (71).

What Peleg hints at here is that those who stray from the true spirit of whaling, who engage in the hunt for worldly, selfish purposes, will suffer the loss of their "standpoint" or leg, symbolic of the phallus or life force, as the captain of the *Pequod* does. It seems hardly a coincidence that, when Peleg hears of such heresy, he suspects Ishmael of being a kind of parricide, accusing him of thinking about "murdering the officers" when he gets to sea. To be sure, Peleg is stringing him along, playing him for the greenhorn he is, as Ishmael eventually comes to realize. But when he returns to the questioning in earnest, asking about Ishmael's motives in wanting to go "a-whaling," Peleg begins to see a

little into his heart, and what he finds wins him over to the novice's side: "Well, sir, I want to see what whaling is," Ishmael replies. "I want to see the world" (71). Demonstrating the simple curiosity and innocent wonder of the true aspirant, Ishmael here reveals none of the covetousness or sensualism typical of the men in the merchant service, and none of the egotism that will later emerge in Ahab. After more of Peleg's tough questioning, which Ishmael gets through with relative ease, he is invited "below deck into the cabin," there to sign the ship's papers, and to meet Bildad, in the last test of this early series (73).

Bildad is made of sterner stuff than Peleg, however, and poses a stiffer challenge. Originally "educated according to the strictest sect of Nantucket Quakerism," he is a man who in his later years has resisted all the world's temptations, even "the sight of many unclad, lovely island creatures, round the Horn," as Ulysses resisted the sirens. Known chiefly for his "immutableness," he is one who has himself passed the true whaleman's test, and as such he is thus best suited to administer it to others (74). Like an old sachem or rabbi confronting a young initiate, he asks Ishmael just a single question, composed of two well-chosen words. So masterful is this high priest of whaling—who throughout the interview sits holding the Scriptures in his hands—that he formulates his query using the words of his friend, simply redirecting them to this supplicant. When Peleg informs him that Ishmael says "he's our man, . . . he wants to ship," Bildad masterfully turns to the would-be hero and asks him to testify on his own behalf, "Dost thee?" He thus puts to him the one essential question: he asks Ishmael to search his heart and speak his fitness for signing on. That Ishmael speaks truly when he replies "I *dost*" is attested to by the fact that in doing so he slips into the idiom of the old Quaker whaleman, exemplar of Nantucket's great adventurers, and that he does so "unconsciously." For as is repeatedly revealed in *Moby-Dick,* to speak unconsciously is to speak out of the authority of the divine self. In saying "I *dost,*" Ishmael does more than assert his readiness, however. He also proclaims his own mortality and thus confesses his dependence on the divine energy to sustain him: "I am dust," he seems to say. At the end of their brief interview, then, Ishmael receives Bildad's laconic blessing or approval. When Peleg asks his friend what he thinks of their young prospect, Bildad responds only with a slightly exasperated but neatly ambiguous, "He'll do" (75).

That Bildad also proves to be exceedingly tight-fisted when it comes to assigning Ishmael his share of the ship's profits may not be so much a sign of hypocrisy in the end, as is generally thought, as it is a sign of consistency. Bildad does have a weaker side, but a case can also be made that he drives a hard bargain because he knows that any worldiness, any sign of hunger for "a princely fortune" (76), may so contaminate the initiate's efforts as to lead him to ruin.

Bildad knows that the initiate must put all ideas of making an earthly fortune out of his mind if he is to have any hope of gaining the ultimate reward. As he says, "where your treasure is, there will your heart be also" (77). Indeed, one's heart, or soul, as Melville explains throughout *Moby-Dick,* is one's treasure.

Having affirmed his readiness for the voyage of the *Pequod,* Ishmael is now prepared to speak the name of the "I" who uttered "I *dost.*" Returning to his room in the Try-Pots Inn, where Queequeg has been observing his "Ramadan," practicing the sort of asceticism or indifference to the world that Bildad had been trying to instill in Ishmael, Ishmael tries to rouse the Polynesian by speaking softly through the keyhole. In doing so, he announces his identity for the first time in the chronology of the book's events. "Queequeg," he whispers, as though still seeking some external confirmation of himself. "I say, Queequeg! why don't you speak? It's I—Ishmael" (82). Ironically, at the very moment he wants Queequeg to confirm his presence, Ishmael is giving voice to his own deepest self. Here, for the first time, we can begin to appreciate the significance of Ishmael's name, which in Hebrew means "God shall hear," for the biblical Ishmael was more than an outcast or rejected son; he was also one whose name contained the promise of divine redemption. To identify oneself as "Ishmael" is to speak one's faith that the self contains within it all the strength of God the Father. Of course, Queequeg, who is both a simple savage from Kokovoko and an image of the eternal soul within each person, does not stir until he is ready. The soul will not respond simply because it is summoned. At times we may assume that it will succumb to our "polite arts and blandishments," as Ishmael wrongly assumes Queequeg will do in this same scene (84). But generally it comes alive in its own good time, according to a rhythm of its own, as Queequeg finally does the next morning, long after Ishmael has given up trying to rouse him, and the sun first enters their room.

Brief as this scene is, Ishmael nonetheless shows that he has learned to respect the independence of the soul that bides its time. Confident, finally, that Queequeg will eventually follow him to bed, Ishmael takes his own bearskin jacket and, in his last act before retiring, throws it over his new friend, "as it promised to be a very cold night" (84). It is not a gesture that shows much respect for the savage's own wishes, to be sure. But it is an act of real tenderness just the same, one that shows Ishmael to have made a big advance over the smug tolerance he had claimed at the start of this chapter.

As if to confirm that at least a small opening has been made in Ishmael's religious temper, the chapter ends with a reversal of the beginning. Instead of congratulating himself for his noblesse oblige, as he did when he first met Queequeg and learned of his bizarre religious practices, he ends with the sudden recognition that an illiterate savage like Queequeg was capable of feeling much the same way toward himself, thinking that "he knew a good deal more about the true religion than I did" and felt "a sort of condescending concern and compassion" for Ishmael because of his great ignorance (86). Thus, while Ishmael opens the chapter with only a tiny "key-hole prospect" onto Queequeg's Ramadan (and a "crooked and sinister one" at that, as he says), he ends it with the light of day finally dawning on him, literally and figuratively (82). Still a good Presbyterian, garrulously proselytizing to Queequeg even in the last paragraphs of this chapter, Ishmael at least shows signs of becoming more understanding of the religious beliefs and practices of his companion and of learning to appreciate the universal conditions underlying the world's many religions.

Having grown more tolerant himself, now, the naturally loquacious Ishmael finds it but a small step to preaching toleration to others. Chapter 18, "His Mark," ostensibly concerns Queequeg's demonstration of prowess with a harpoon (hitting "his mark") and signing the ship's papers (making "his mark"). But, less obviously, it also concerns Ishmael's growing ecumenicalism, even to the point of showing him in the outrageously funny, unexpected role of Queequeg's evangelist—not his Matthew, Luke, or John, but "His Mark." From the time he enters the story, Queequeg has been something of a Christ-figure to Ishmael, prompting his spiritual awakening, guiding the recovery of his soul, pointing the way to renewed health and happiness. Of course there is a good deal of leg-pulling in Ishmael's exorbitant claim to the Quaker captains that "Queequeg here is a born member of the First Congregational Church. He is a deacon himself, Queequeg is" (88). But beneath the humor of his prevarication and wordplay, the gospel truth of Ishmael's universalism shines through.

Contrary to those, such as H. Bruce Franklin, who argue that *Moby-Dick* shows Melville's preoccupation with one or another religious mythology, I would emphasize the importance of Ishmael's growing ecumenicalism, an ecumenicalism that reaches its high point in this scene. Pressed hard by Bildad to explain himself, Ishmael responds facetiously, "I mean, sir, the same ancient Catholic Church to which you and I, and Captain Peleg there, and Queequeg here, and all of us, and every mother's son and soul of us belong; the great and everlasting First Congregation of this whole worshipping world; we all belong to that . . . in *that* we all join hands." "Splice, thou mean'st *splice* hands," Peleg corrects him, thus emphasizing his own recognition, under the sway of Ishmael's rhetoric, of the powerful human bonds, the equality and goodwill, that everyone celebrates in the simple gesture of joining hands (later celebrated in "A Squeeze of the Hand"). Ironically, it is Peleg, then, and not Queequeg, who comes to be converted in this chapter. His heart is changed by the upstart evangelist Ishmael, as he himself humorously confesses. "Young man," Peleg exclaims, at the same time telling them to forget about the cannibal's so-called "conversion" papers and inviting the two of them on board, "you'd better ship for a missionary, instead of a fore-mast hand; I never heard a better sermon" (88).

Bildad is not so easily won over, however. "Eyeing" Queequeg during the signing of the *Pequod*'s papers, afterward he stands and places a tract entitled "The Latter Day Coming; or No Time to Lose," in the cannibal's hands. Only then does he join hands with him, grasping both the little book and Queequeg's hands in his own. Looking "earnestly into his eyes," he warns him to "mind thine eye" and "turn from the wrath to come." But clearly these are wasted words, like the words in the tract that the illiterate Queequeg will never read (nor needs to). As the incarnation of the soul, Queequeg has no ego involvement in the life he leads; unlike Ahab, he does not have to mind his "I." Neither does he have to concern himself with the Last Things, for he has nothing to lose in the end. Instead, as demonstrated earlier, Queequeg keeps his eye on the eye of the whale, the incarnation of the self. For the whale is an image of all Nature, what Emerson called the "Other Me." Like a Buddhist archer, who trains himself to think of nothing but his target, Queequeg is a perfect master, one who can hit the "spot" at will, because he and the whale's eye are one (88–89).

Elijah, the "Prophet" of the next chapter, mysteriously materializes to provide Ishmael his final test before he ships out, asking him whether he has any fear for his soul and darkly hinting that he has committed himself to a fatal undertaking. As the last guardian of the threshold to the magic realm, the prophet tries to shake the initiate's resolve by casting doubt on the ship's whole enterprise; by claiming to know all about its strange past and the captain he enigmaticly refers to as "Old Thunder"; and by pretending to have knowledge of the *Pequod*'s future (92). After determining that Ishmael and his friend have just signed the ship's articles, the old sailor inquires ominously, "Anything down there about your souls?" Ironically, Ishmael seems not to comprehend: "About what?" he replies (91). In this case, he is fortunate not to understand Elijah, for we see here by how thin a thread the fate of the would-be adventurer hangs; if Ishmael had comprehended the old prophet, he might have been scared away, or so we are led to assume. However, Ishmael does continue to resist Elijah's sly insinuations, and in the end the old man intimates that Ishmael is made of the true stuff: "I like to hear a chap talk up that way," he says, pretending to call an end to their talk; "you are just the man for him [i.e., Ahab]—the likes of ye. Morning to ye, shipmates, morning!" (93). Despite some lingering doubts after he learns the name of this stranger,

Ishmael dismisses them almost entirely by the end of the scene, just a trace of uncertainty remaining to show his mortality.

In the concluding three chapters of this long opening section of *Moby-Dick,* Melville brings to a close the themes of the preparation for the hunt that are his chief concern. "All Astir," which focuses on the preparation of the ship—the purchasing and collecting and the fetching, hauling, and stowing down of its stores—conveys the idea of the world's richness or fecundity, its boundless capacity to provide for the hero's material needs so he can get on with the important business of the quest. Like Mother Nature, the figure called Aunt Charity, who is the *Pequod*'s chief provisioner, is "a lean old lady of a most determined and indefatigable spirit, but withal very kindhearted." She is an image of the eternal woman, always up and doing, forever eager to lend her "hand and heart to anything that promised to yield safety, comfort, and consolation" to the ship's officers and crew. But, even so, there are some needs that even the eternal female cannot supply, some accidents or losses she cannot anticipate or protect against. While the whale ship has been provisioned with "spare boats, spare spars, and spare lines and harpoons, and spare everythings, almost," there can be no supplying, as Ishmael says with both humor and seriousness, of a "spare Captain and duplicate ship" (96). For some things, the men must supply their own insurance; they must be their own protection. How they might accomplish that all-important task is the subject of the next chapter, "Going Aboard," the title of which reiterates a timeless call to adventure.

The next day, when Ishmael and Queequeg make their way past crazy Elijah one last time and step aboard the *Pequod,* it is still early morning, and all is quiet, "not a soul moving." The only person they encounter is a sleeper, a man down in the forecastle spread "at whole length upon two chests" [a fore-image of Ishmael on the coffin/life-buoy at the end], "his face downwards and inclosed in his folded arms," a pose symbolizing self-protection. An old rigger, "wrapped in a tattered pea-jacket," a variation of the earlier image of Queequeg at his Ramadan with Ishmael's coat thrown over him, this curious figure is another likeness of the soul, but the soul in a state of sleep (99). Taking seats at each end of the man, Ishmael and Queequeg pass the time talking and sharing a smoke from the latter's odd tomahawk-pipe. Unaccountably, whenever Queequeg took his turn with the instrument, "he flourished the hatchet-side of it over the sleeper's head," and when Ishmael asks what he is up to, he says only, "Perry easy, kill-e; oh! perry easy!" Still, the action and the explanation together make it clear that Queequeg is acting out a version of the story of Damocles, and that in his version the sword of Fate hangs over the soul that sleeps. The soul must never let down its guard. Like the sleeper who finally wakes to the smoke of his own damnation, the soul must be "all alive now"; it must "turn to." It, too, must be forever up and about its business (100).

What that business consists of Ishmael unwittingly explains when he says that Queequeg's tomahawk-pipe "both brained his foes and soothed his soul" (100). Quite simply, it is the soul's job to slay its enemies; only then can it feel "soothed."[22] In fact, such a notion of the soul's duty provides the rationale for the rest of Melville's epic story. It explains why Ishmael, having found his deepest self, must still go to sea—not to slay the White Whale (which is, after all, Melville's great image of the soul) but to destroy its enemies. Despite this long foreground, then, the journey of Ishmael is only now ready to begin.

At various times in the land-based chapters of *Moby-Dick,* Ishmael shows that he is a fearful man, as well as a man of courage. Whether making his way through the pitch-black streets of New Bedford or facing the prospect of sleeping with a savage; whether contemplating the cenotaphs in the Whaleman's Chapel or standing helplessly outside Queequeg's locked room, Ishmael evidences a nervous, morbid imagination. He is a man who fears death and destruction, and premature burial most of all. In the chapters at the end of this section, his fearfulness even intensifies, as he comes closer and closer to the time when he must cross the threshold of the ship for the last time and move irreversibly into Captain Ahab's domain. The first meeting with Elijah stirs up in Ishmael "all kinds of vague wonderments and half-apprehensions" concerning the *Pequod,* its mysterious captain, and the leg he has lost; and when he sees a group of dim, shadowy figures boarding the ship before dawn the next morning, he has to "beat . . . down" his fear when he learns they are nowhere to be found. Significantly, it "seemed," Ishmael says, that "Queequeg had not at all noticed" these strange figures (93, 99). Undoubtedly Queequeg did notice them, and everything else besides. The reason he seems not to observe such things is simply that he has no fears, and so he registers no reactions. Unlike the young Ishmael, he is always the master of himself. In the chapter titled "Merry Christmas," when the *Pequod* is making its way out to sea, Ishmael is given a lesson to this effect, a Christmas present in the form of a swift kick in the pants from Captain Peleg, who commands the ship while it is headed out to sea. Ironically, then, even at the start of his quest, Ishmael is offered a "boon," one of the most valuable to be gleaned from his whole journey. Having stopped in the midst of his sailor duties to worry about the perils of starting the voyage with "such a devil for a pilot" as Peleg, who had taken to shouting out his orders in great oaths, Ishmael feels a "sudden sharp poke in my rear"—a timely warning that he needs to pay attention to his duty and not to his fears (103). Clearly, this is a lesson Ishmael takes to heart, for he is never kicked a second time, not even, in the end, by Moby Dick.

"The Lee Shore" is the capstone (a substitute, Ishmael intimates, for a tombstone) of the long opening section of *Moby-Dick* that is so thoroughly permeated by themes of death and burial. A memorial to the questing spirit incarnated in Bulkington, the mariner who hardly lands from one voyage before embarking on another, this chapter offers the promise that the adventuring hero never really dies and is never really buried. "Wonderfullest things are ever the unmentionable," Ishmael exclaims concerning the apparent immortality of this eternally restless figure; "deep memories yield no epitaphs; this six-inch chapter is the stoneless grave of Bulkington" (106). It is important that Ishmael mentions Bulkington as a future "sleeping-partner" of his (16), for like the old rigger whom Ishmael and Queequeg found sleeping in the forecastle on the morning of their departure, Bulkington is next seen "all alive" and tending to business up on the deck, indeed "standing at her helm." What makes Bulkington such a remarkable instance of the adventuring hero is not simply that he can put his fears behind him, as Peleg would have Ishmael do, but that he can put all of his needs for every kind of human comfort behind him as well. As his example suggests, the quest is the most strenuous undertaking imaginable, requiring the most heroic discipline and great personal sacrifice. Like the "storm-tossed ship, that miserably drives along the leeward land," all the power of nature seems to force the quester such as Bulkington toward the shore, the land of his mortal being, inviting him to find rest in comforts that are falsely soothing, or in a peace known only to the dead. "The port would fain give succor; the port is pitiful; in the port is safety, comfort, hearthstone, supper, warm blankets, friends, all that's kind to our mortalities," Ishmael explains. But in that gale, until the agitated adventurer finds true peace, until he slays his enemies, "the port, the land, is that ship's direst jeopardy." Just "one touch of land" would mean instant destruction (106).

Thus all adventuring, Ishmael argues, "all deep, earnest thinking is but the intrepid effort of *the soul* to keep the open independence of her sea; while the wildest winds of heaven and earth conspire to cast her on the treacherous, slavish shore" (emphasis added). Though the quester cannot know while in the midst of his adventure whether he will ever reach his goal, ever slay his enemies or come face to face with the Father, "better is it to perish in that howling infinite [of landlessness], than be ingloriously dashed upon the lee, even if that were safety!" Even so, Ishmael insists, speaking now as one who has already lived through the adventure and, like Queequeg, knows the result to be a truly divine translation, the "agony" of the journey, and the "terrors" of the trial, are not "vain." "Take heart, take heart, O Bulkington! Bear thee grimly, demigod! Up from the spray of thy ocean-perishing—straight up, leaps thy apotheosis!" (107). As in other spiritual epics, Ishmael suggests, the hero will eventually come to appreciate the apparent paradox that in his death is his life. Only by dying to the world, only by being tried in the belly of the whale endlessly, can he hope to experience the continuous rebirth of the soul that keeps it vital.

II. THE GAME OF CHESS

In "The Advocate," which in the chronology of the story appears after the *Pequod* has reached sea, Ishmael suddenly begins to speak in a new voice. Jumping way ahead and looking back on his life retrospectively, he is now an experienced whaleman addressing an audience of the uninitiated, instructing his readers in the complexities of the whale fishery. He thus begins to speak consistently for the first time as an epic poet, who, as E. M. W. Tillyard has said, combines "abundant content and masterly control," or breadth of knowledge and density of language.[23] Because whaling seems so unpromising and unlikely a subject for an epic, so "unpoetical and disreputable," Ishmael must become an aggressive "advocate." But in doing so he deviates only in tone—exaggerated, straining after effect, comic—from the role of the traditional epic poet such as Homer or Milton, whose job it is to mediate between the lives of his heroes and his audience, explaining to us their arcane activities; promoting their enterprise; and in general trying to make us see that we have an investment in their cause. Like the master of an intricate sport, such as whale fishing can be, he must also instruct his readers in the rules of the game.

However, if he is to convince those readers to take up the game themselves, he must do more than explain how it is played. He must portray the men who are its champions and communicate something of the spirit of their peculiar activity. He must engage the interest of his readers in the lives of exemplary heroes who are themselves caught up in a quintessential contest, and he must raise the stature and importance of their undertaking so that the universal destiny will be seen to be symbolized in their experience. That, more than anything else, according to Abercrombie, is the principal task of the epic poet, and that is what Ishmael attempts to do in chapter 24 and in the several chapters that follow.[24]

Because the whalemen and their legendary antagonist, the great White Whale, must be introduced to the reader and their histories brought up to date; and because, too, the life on an American whaleship needs to be portrayed, this second section of *Moby-Dick* is more essay than narrative. Opening not with one or two but half a dozen or more chapters cast in a polemical style, including speculative chapters on "Cetology" and "The Whiteness of the Whale," the second part of Melville's epic novel closes, appropriately, at the end of "The Mat-Maker," chapter 47, another speculative chapter, where Ishmael's effort to weave the forces of fate, free will, and chance into a single cosmic theory is unexpectedly interrupted by the sighting of the *Pequod*'s first whale. With the sounding of the whaleman's "There she blows!," Ishmael suddenly realizes that the business of whaling is a thing of destiny. For when the brute fact of the whale abruptly surfaces to interrupt the flow of Ishmael's imagination, "the ball of free will dropped from my hand" (215). And the mat, like the theory it symbolizes, is left behind, unfinished.

Given the inherently unpromising nature of his subject, Melville had to go to great lengths to achieve the epic effect of significance in portraying his chief actors. Heroic action requires heroic characters, and the whalemen are widely thought to be nothing more than "butchers" (108). However, Ishmael, who manages time and again to turn obstacles into challenges to his inventiveness, immediately sets about appropriating epic conventions to his own needs, arguing, for example, with tongue firmly in his cheek, that martial commanders, who are among the most common heroes of epic, have themselves often been the bloodiest butchers in the world. Whatever reservations one might conceive of regarding the fitness of whalemen to serve as heroes for an epic, Ishmael has a mock-logical counterargument. If it is thought that whaling has no power or influence in the ways of the world, or that it has never had a redeeming "peaceful" or civilizing influence on the course of history, he counters with little-known facts showing how fabulously lucrative the whaling enterprise has been, or with outlandish examples of countries, or entire continents, that have been liberated from colonialism through the efforts of the early whalemen (109).

In rejoinder after rejoinder, example after historical example, Ishmael builds a hyperbolic case for the nobility of the whale, for the dignity of the whaling business, and even for the royalty of the whaling man's blood. Repeatedly he calls up outrageous analogies from royal history or custom to place his whaling material in the heroic tradition, as he does, most memorably, when he speaks of the coronation of the heads of kings in terms of oiling a "head of salad" with whale oil (113). Among the most important analogies are the several provided in the two "Knights and Squires" chapters, which elevate the *Pequod*'s motley mates and harpooneers to the level of Arthurian aristocrats, or at least attempt to. And Ishmael does much the same thing in the next chapter, which focuses on Ahab, the crotchety Nantucket captain named for a wicked Old Testament king. Melville has even managed to insert a queen into the dramatis personae introduced here, namely, "Queen Mab" (the subject of chapter 31), the fairy queen of English folklore believed to govern people's dreams.

As the mocking tone of "Postscript," chapter 25, suggests, however, and as Ishmael matter-of-factly maintains at the end of the first "Knights and Squires" chapter, the concern with royalty in the epic genre, the preoccupation with titles and bloodlines and pomp, is a concern merely with the trappings, rather than the essence, of the epic story. Anticipating his portrayal of the sorrowful "fall of valor in the soul" of Starbuck, when the first mate tries to stand up to Ahab, Ishmael states that "this august dignity I treat of, is not the dignity of kings and robes, but that abounding dignity which has no robed investiture." In oxymoronic language characteristic of the epic, Ishmael describes his subject as "that democratic dignity which, on all hands, radiates without end from God; Himself!" He observes that God calls His "selectest champions," including such notorious popular examples as John Bunyan and Andrew Jackson, from "the kingly commons." Repeatedly in these chapters, it is natural, self-made courage, not inherited rank or wealth, that forms the basis of such dignity, in Ishmael's view, and that makes even these "meanest mariners, and renegades and castaways" who serve on the *Pequod* worthy of epic treatment (117). Starbuck possesses such courage, though for him it is "a thing simply useful" in the hunting of whales (116). And Stubb and Flask do, too, though on a lower plane, the one being simply "indifferent" and the other "dead" to any apprehensions of danger (118–19). The higher forms of courage, on the other hand, simple daring and coolness under pressure, are represented in the three harpooneers, Queequeg, Tashtego, and Daggoo, and in the *Pequod*'s captain, who is portrayed memorably the first time we see him, staring out beyond the ship's bow with "an infinity of firmest fortitude, a determinate, unsurrenderable wilfulness," in his search for Moby Dick (124).

All of these examples are early signs that Melville was working self-consciously in the epic tradition, a tradition increasingly recognized as being self-consciousnessly imitative, as Tom Winnifrith has argued, or parodic, as John Kevin Newman has said.[25] In all the major epics, whether oral or literary, the most conspicuous value is simply courage. All the great epics, as Abercrombie has explained, remind us that, while courage may not be the only significant attitude one can hold toward life, "man can achieve nothing until he has first achieved courage." Given the precariousness of life, particularly when the oral epics were being formed, it follows that courage is "the absolutely necessary foundation of any subsequent valuation of life," and so it proved to be, even in the development of the spiritual epic.[26]

More than any other character, Ahab dominates the second part of *Moby-Dick*. As "supreme lord and dictator" of the *Pequod* and the protagonist in Melville's story of the Whale, he is also, of course, the book's central character (122). However, he is not Melville's example of the epic hero, the redemptive figure of universal mythology. That role has been reserved for Ishmael. Instead, Ahab is Melville's example of the failed hero, the man who refuses the call to adventure. He is the opposite of Melville's narrator, not an incarnation of the self, or soul, but of the selfish ego. Like Minos, the Cretan in Ovid's *Metamorphoses,* a work that at least one critic has called an epic,[27] Ahab is a ruler who forsakes his public duty for his private need and is thus transformed into a tyrant. Rather than serve the group he has been entrusted to lead, he uses his position to force the group to serve him, as Melville makes plain in "The Specksynder" (chapter 33). And in the process he brings everything to ruin.

A psychologically complex figure, "fear-haunted" yet hostile, "alert at every hand to meet and battle back the anticipated aggressions of his environment," the "tyrant-monster," as Campbell calls such a figure, is "the world's messenger of disaster, even though, in his mind, he may entertain himself with humane intentions."[28] Such a man is Ahab, who also believes his aggression is the product of high purpose and in the end brings catastrophe to himself and his men. In his imagination, he "piled upon the whale's white hump the sum of all the general rage and hate felt by his whole race from Adam down" and then set himself the insuperable task of eradicating all evil from the world (184). But his professed intention masks his private fear and hatred. The evil he sees in Moby Dick is a projection, mainly, out of the hell of his own psyche.

Everything about Ahab, as Ishmael initially presents him, hints at his being a man who has repeatedly refused the call to the soul's awakening and who, instead of submitting to the will of God, holds ever more tightly to the little bit of mortality allotted to him. On his first entrance, he is described as one who has somehow escaped a trial by fire but been scarred by it, not as one who calmly submitted and proved himself equal to it: "He looked," as Ishmael says, "like a man cut away from the stake, when the fire has overrunningly wasted all the limbs without consuming them." Of the thin, rodlike mark running down the side of Ahab's face, Ishmael says it resembled the seam in a great tree trunk after a lightning bolt (symbol of Zeus, of the deity) has ripped through it, "leaving the tree still greenly alive, but branded" (123). Only after he has examined these sinister details does Ishmael even notice Ahab's "barbaric white leg," the book's overriding symbol, and symptom, of Ahab's dying and of his inevitable return to the dust he came from. And only then, almost by way of explanation, does he observe that the "moody stricken" Ahab carries the look of a "crucifixion" in his face, emblem of the would-be redeemer who has lost faith and feels himself forsaken by his God (124).

In fact, in the concluding paragraphs of this chapter Ishmael underscores the fact that Ahab has been near death, not only from his recent wound but also from the ravages of age and winter. As the *Pequod* sails south, therefore, into spring and the whale's customary feeding grounds, Ahab comes up on deck more and more, his face each time more alive, like a "thunder-cloven old oak" that at last sends forth "some few green sprouts" (125). Summoned back for one last meeting with the Father, Ahab believes he is on a mission of destruction that will guarantee him a kind of immortality. Only later will he come to admit his fear that he is the one who will be destroyed. As in the spiritual epics of Dante and Milton, and indeed in all the great religious mythologies of the world, Ahab's refusal of the invitation to come home to God is a refusal to give up his limited, earthly conception of what constitutes his own self-interest. Like the heroes of these other works, he looks at the future not in terms of death and rebirth, but as a relentless threat to his vitality, to his identity and everything he stands for.[29] So fearful of death is he, so desperate to cling to the life he still holds, that soon after his first appearance on deck, as the ship moves into the tropics, he grows reluctant to leave the open air, even at night, and go down to his cabin for sleep: "It feels like going down into one's tomb," he would mutter to himself, ". . . to go to my grave-dug berth" (127).

Fearful of death, ever sensitive to insult, resistant to loss or change, Ahab is incapable of taking even a step, let alone a leap, into the unknown. Indeed, so rigid is he that he contests to the death any will that challenges his own. To the man like Ahab who lives in time, locked in the grasp of the ego, even the divinity becomes an enemy. "Talk not to me of blasphemy, man," he exclaims to Starbuck, when the first mate questions his motives for going after Moby Dick; "I'd strike the sun if it insulted me" (164). He refuses to see that life perpetually enacts the mystery of dismemberment, even as it enacts also the mystery of renewal. Speaking as though he considered his own dismasting to be a unique occurrence rather than but one instance of the common fate, Ahab reminds himself that the "prophecy was that I should be dismembered," and then he tries to bolster his ego by pretending to play prophet himself, claiming boldly that "I now prophesy that I will dismember my dismemberer" (168). He does not understand, what an anonymous Long Island sailor perceives when the latter says enigmatically, in "Midnight, Forecastle" (Chapter 40), "Hoe corn when you may, say I. All legs go to harvest soon" (174).

Despite his blasphemy, Ahab is otherwise a glorious figure, the representative man of his time, the American at midcentury. As the book's epic hero manqué, he contains within him not only the common, universal values of his type but Melville's summation of the cultural values of the United States in 1850—pride, independence, manly determination, pragmatism. These are not the highest values, to be sure, and they are not the only ones found in nineteenth-century America, but they are the predominant ones. So, too, Ahab's greatness is a "mortal greatness," a greatness that is "disease," and not the immortal kind that Ishmael comes to exemplify (74). Though Ahab is a powerfully sympathetic figure, it is clear Melville himself did not subscribe to the values he embodies. On the contrary, he saw them as America's doom. What Melville perceived, in looking at the young nation, was a whole culture trapped, as Emerson had said, in the temporal dimension of life; incapable of throwing off the childish ego; sensitive to any threat to its interests, big or small; quick to defend its sovereignty as well as its honor; lacking any real faith in the unseen, the spirit world of the soul, to sustain life and give it transcendent meaning.

Repeatedly in this second part of *Moby-Dick,* Melville portrays characters trading insults, plotting revenge, eagerly jumping into senseless fights, as they do at the end of the long dramatic chapter 40, when a Spanish sailor, bearing some nameless "old grudge," provokes a row with Daggoo by using a sly racial epithet (177). As timely, even culture-bound, as Melville's portrayal of the representative man is, however, it is also timeless, universal, as even this small example of the Spanish sailor suggests. As an old Manx sailor exclaims, in response to a call for the crew to form a ring around the combatants, "Ready formed. There! the ringed horizon. In that ring Cain struck Abel. Sweet work, right work! No? Why then, God, mad'st thou the ring?" (178).

From the start of the *Pequod*'s journey, when Stubb ventures to ask Ahab to muffle his step and Ahab sends him packing, Melville portrays life among the men on ship as a contest of wills, a struggle for supremacy and the spoils of privilege. In the everyday affairs described in "The Specksynder" (chapter 33), and more particularly in "The Cabin-Table" (chapter 34), a symbolic scene in which the captain presides over the apportionment of every dish, Ahab carefully maintains his position by observing the "forms and usages" of the sea. At times he does "mask" his true intentions, as Ishmael explains, "incidentally making use of [these common practices] for other and more private ends than they were legitimately intended to subserve" (147). Ahab does this most obviously in "The Quarter-Deck" (chapter 36), where, to bind the crew to his mad plan, he promises a gold doubloon to the man who first sights Moby Dick and then beats down, by sheer force of will, the first mate's objections. No matter how superior a man's intellect, Ishmael observes in "The Specksynder," he can never assume a position of practical advantage over others "without the aid of some sort of external arts and entrenchments, always, in themselves, more or less paltry and base." This, as Ishmael goes on to explain in a resonant line, is what "for ever keeps God's true princes of the Empire from the world's hustings; and leaves the highest honors that this air can give, to those men who become famous more through their infinite inferiority to the choice hidden handful of the Divine Inert, than through their undoubted superiority over the dead level of the mass" (148).

This is not to say that the man of soul must forever remain above it all, silently contemplating "the problem of the universe," as Ishmael says he does whenever he takes his turn as lookout (158). He recognizes, at the end of chapter 35, that one must eventually come down from the mast-head and live in the world. There is work to be done, often aggressive, murderous work, in the service of truth and in defense of the soul. But as Stubb's dream makes clear, there is a way of living in the world without being entirely of it, without returning insult for insult or demanding "an eye for an eye" each time one feels he has been wounded. As the fairy queen of English folklore who governs people's dreams, Queen Mab speaks the wisdom of the unconscious, the deeper self. And what she says, in effect, is that there is a passive, Christ-like response to a wounding experience that can prove more sensible, and healing, than the furiously vengeful one demanded by the ego.

When Stubb wakes up the next morning after Ahab has ordered him "Down, dog, and kennel," he tells Flask he had a "queer dream" in which the captain kicked him with his ivory leg, "and when I tried to kick back, *upon my soul* . . . I kicked my leg right off! And then, presto! Ahab seemed a pyramid, and I, *like a blazing fool,* kept kicking at it" (127, 131; emphasis added). To be sure, it is Stubb's ego that views Ahab's outburst of the night before as an insult, just as it is his ego that prompts him, in his dream, to try to return the indignity by kicking back. But as seen when Stubb loses his own leg in his dream—a loss that informs Ahab's dismemberment by Moby Dick—any attempt to avenge an insult against a truly superior power is foolish; it is to stub one's toe on a pyramid, to squander one's potency and harm oneself unnecessarily.

This idea is made more emphatically in what Stubb calls the "greatest joke" of his whole dream, when a hump-backed old merman offers his own posterior as an alternative target for Stubb's kicking. Once the old man turns away, revealing that "his stern was stuck full of marlinspikes, with the points out," the light begins to dawn on "wise Stubb" that he will only hurt *himself* if he keeps kicking (132). But given that he goes back to kicking the pyramid, it is clear he does not see what the image of the inverted marlinspikes really suggests, namely, that the instruments of vengeance will surely be turned back against the aggressor, particularly if wielded out of hate and not out of duty. Such wisdom is finally beyond Stubb, the man whose eleventh commandment is "think not" (128), just as it is finally beyond Ahab, the man who eventually comes to believe that "to think's audacity" (563).

What is also beyond Stubb is that he should change his view of the beating he had taken from Ahab and think of it instead as a source of "great glory." "Remember what I say," the old dream figure tells him before disappearing; "*be* kicked by him; account his kicks honors; and on no account kick back; for you can't help yourself, wise Stubb. Don't you see that pyramid?" (132). Significantly, Stubb shows some potential for change in the brief moment after his encounter with Ahab. While making his way below deck, a stray thought, an unconscious insight into Ahab's true condition as a man of suffering, breaks through his ego's defenses, and he suddenly wonders whether he should go back and strike Ahab or possibly get down and pray for him, though "it would be the first time I ever *did* pray" (128). Stubb, however, never recognizes that what he takes to be an insult may in fact be the mysterious operation of a wise Providence working through his tormentor. And in his failure he mirrors, as his example helps to explain, Ahab's still grander failure.

For Ishmael, the true hero of Melville's story, the crucial question is not whether he can contain his anger and vengefulness, but whether he can resist Ahab and the temptation to make Ahab's feud his own. If he is to have a chance at the epic experience of being swallowed by the whale, he must keep from being swallowed up in Ahab's rage, as all the others are. For a time, however, Ishmael does succumb. As he says at the opening of "Moby Dick" (chapter 41), after the quarterdeck ceremony wherein Ahab impels his men to join in the hunt for the White Whale, "I, Ishmael, was one of that crew; my shouts had gone up with the rest; my oath had been welded with theirs. . . . A wild, mystical, sympathetical feeling was in me; Ahab's quenchless feud seemed mine." The "dread" he admits to feeling "in my soul" during the ceremony, therefore, is caused by his unconscious fear of Ahab, and not by any fear of Moby Dick (155).

With Ahab now established as the greatest challenge to the well-being of his soul, Ishmael has entered into the second, or "purification," stage of the hero's journey, when, as Campbell says, "the senses are 'cleansed and humbled,' and the energies and interests 'concentrated upon transcendental things,'" as they are in "The Mast-Head," one of the key chapters in this part of *Moby-Dick*. In psychological terms, this is the time when the powerful, ruling images of the hero's infantile past are finally confronted and defeated or exorcised, as Ishmael can be seen struggling, throughout the middle three sections of the book, to free himself from Ahab, his domineering "double."[30] Certainly in the beginning, when Ishmael admits to a compulsion to stepping into the street and "methodically knocking people's hats off" (3), he is already a man of rage like the *Pequod*'s captain. It is an easy step for him, then, when the opportunity presents itself, to transfer all his psychic turmoil to a powerful figure like Ahab, who promises to redirect it toward a single, practically assailable target. It should be added, however, that given the passionate response of the crew generally in the quarterdeck scene, the *Pequod*'s captain is not to be viewed as something dredged up out of Ishmael's psyche alone. Ahab is a universal figure, an image of the infantile rage, and hunger, deep within us all.

Intuitively, Ishmael knows that Ahab will present the greatest trial of his entire journey, and he knows this, if only dimly, from the moment he first lays eyes on him. In "Ahab" (chapter 28), where Ishmael describes the portentous moment when he sees the *Pequod*'s captain for the first time, he admits that "foreboding shivers ran over me" (123). In fact, his response to the physical presence of the man is precisely like that of the innocent Vermont colt (described in "The Whiteness of the Whale" chapter) to the shaking of a buffalo skin from the western prairie—an unpremeditated, reflex action to a mysterious but palpable threat of death. Significantly, Ishmael experiences no such fear when he first sights a whale, not even when he first sights Moby Dick on the final day of the chase. In the single moment of Ishmael's first view of Ahab is epitomized the central problem of the second part of the hero's epic journey, when he is captured, or seduced, by his opposite, his repressed self or ego-image.

In the early days of the *Pequod*'s journey, when Ishmael is willing to make Ahab's feud his own, it is Ishmael's resistances, not Ahab's, that are broken as he puts aside his pride, his own purpose in signing up for the voyage, and even his own safety and submits to "crazy Ahab's" plan (184). At the point where Ahab's feud becomes his own, Ishmael finds that he and this powerful "double" are one. The key questions of the second part of his journey, then, are whether Ishmael can somehow free himself from the feud of the wounded captain, now that he has been powerfully galvanized by him, and where he will find the force, the self-mastery, to do so.

In the early days of the hunt, Ishmael cannot know that the White Whale will be his salvation. He cannot know that Moby Dick will empower him, by the force and magnitude of its vitalizing effect on his own imagination, to throw off Ahab's rage and resume the course of his own adventure; just as he cannot know that his deeper self will empower him to break the stranglehold of his ego. In the first stage of the journey, while under Ahab's influence, Ishmael takes the position that the whale is fundamentally malicious. In "The Affadavit" (chapter 45), for example, he lends his support to the view that the whale is a creature capable of "wilful, deliberate designs of destruction"(209).

But, as caught up in Ahab's design as he is, Ishmael does not share Ahab's totalizing view that "all evil" is "visibly personified, and made practically assailable," in the great whale (184). His own view is subtler and more elusive, just as his intelligence is rarer and more true. In fact, when in "The Whiteness of the Whale" he attempts to set down what it is that "above all things appalled" him about Moby Dick, Ishmael provides such a searching yet finally uncertain assessment of the subject as to torment his readers with his own sense of bafflement (188). Without being at all sure that what he says is accurate, couching every statement in conditional (or interrogative) terms, Ishmael comes to suspect that it is not the whiteness of the whale he finds so menacing but the indefiniteness of that whiteness—the basal, even existential, meaninglessness of it. What is so appalling to Ishmael about the whale's white color is that it seems to undermine all possibility for faith in the existence of a divine intention or plan in all the operations of the universe. As he haltingly tries to explain, near the end of his long effort to capture his exact feelings,

> Is it that by its indefiniteness it shadows forth the heartless voids and immensities of the universe, and thus stabs us from behind with the thought of annihilation, when beholding the white depths of the milky way? Or is it, that as in essence whiteness is not so much a color as the visible absence of color, and at the same time the concrete of all colors; is it for these reasons that there is such a dumb blankness, full of meaning, in a wide landscape of snows—a colorless, all-color of atheism from which we shrink? (195)

Clearly, in this chapter, where he works so diligently to strip the whale's whiteness of all associations, the positive ones, the negative ones, and those in between, Ishmael senses the wrongheadedness, the subjectivity, of Ahab's view of the whale. But despite his magnificent, epic effort to get at the essence of the matter, Ishmael cannot at this stage get beyond the point of seeing the whale as a hideous blank screen on which every observer projects his own torment. Alert to the contradictions in the whale's whiteness, Ishmael is still incapable of seeing them as coexisting at once in one being. Instead, he concludes that they must have their origin in the subjective consciousness of the observer, each in effect cancelling the other out in a final blank meaninglessness. He is still not prepared to understand the paradoxical character of the whale's whiteness, for he is still not prepared to understand the paradoxical character of his own soul and of the primordial force that governs all life. Though he senses the need to free himself from the monomania of Ahab's view, the best he can do, without supernatural aid, is wonder whether the whiteness of the whale, or by extension the whale itself, has any inherent meaning, any irreducible purpose whatsoever. Having been magnetized by the force of Ahab's personality, and thus having lost touch temporarily with his own all-comprehending soul, Ishmael is incapable of apprehending the dual nature, the good *and* the evil, of Leviathan.

Only in the end, when Ishmael sees Moby Dick for the first time and comes under its life-changing spell, does he have the full power of his own soul restored to him. Then, using his own eyes instead of Ahab's, he can see the whale to be the incarnation of the life-giving dismemberer, the great God Absolute that is both Creator and Destroyer. Only then can he understand that the White Whale is an image of the divine power that inheres in all things, wreaking destruction on the dying generations, bringing life to those waiting to be reborn. As primordial yet fresh an image as any in the world's literature, Melville's whale is finally but a variation of the age-old image of doubleness—the doubleness of God, and of the world that is God's creation. Like the all-devouring monster, the bull-demon of the labyrinth in the myth of Theseus, the great White Whale has one aspect that is angry, provoking, and destructive and another that is benign, enlightening, and vivifying. Simultaneously a figure of doom and of what Campbell calls the "world navel," the whale is Melville's symbol of the source of all existence, of all harm and all beneficence.[31] Like Moby Dick—rumored to be both "ubiquitous" and "immortal"; supplier of light and of life—the world navel is everywhere and everlasting, yet also double, inexhaustibly supplying both sustenance and death, happiness and sorrow, goodness and iniquity (182–83).

Those who fail to understand the doubleness of nature, and of human experience, will necessarily fear death and resist the inevitable process of dismemberment. Like Ahab, they will focus all their attention on the forces that threaten them and feel so hemmed in as to think they inhabit a prison. "How can the prisoner reach outside," Ahab exclaims to Starbuck, in his first major speech, "except by thrusting through the wall? To me, the white whale is that wall, shoved near to me" (164). Ahab's expression of imprisonment is but a trope for the impotence of the ego. For no matter how large, the ego is always limited in power; it cannot penetrate the wall of the material universe. Only the soul, the deeper self, can do that, and "Ahab's soul," we are told at the end of chapter 34, is in effect dead, sleeping away the winter in the hollow of a tree like an old bear "shut up in the caved trunk of his body," feeding on "the sullen paws of its gloom" (153).

Repeatedly, Melville suggests it is when the soul is inactive, sleeping, or "dead" that one is most sensitive to the threat of dismemberment, or most fearful of life. It is, for instance, after Ahab has overpowered Starbuck's resistance in the quarterdeck scene that the first mate confesses, "with soul beat down," that he feels the "latent horror" in life (170). But it is also clear that his soul has been "overmanned," as Starbuck says, not because Ahab is a monster of superior force, but because Starbuck has not trusted his own power to resist him. "I would up heart, were it not like lead," he confesses weakly. "But my whole clock's run down; my heart the all-controlling weight. I have no key to lift again." From that moment, Starbuck is defeated, self-defeated. Contrary to what he believes, he does contain the key within himself; however, he is the virtuous man who would fight the horror in life not with the all-powerful soul but "with the soft feeling of the human in me." In the end, he leaves it to God to "wedge aside" Ahab's "heaven-insulting purpose" (169–70). In doing so, he abdicates his responsibility, and he pays for his failure with his life.

Those who do understand the dual nature of nature will have no fear of death; they will in fact embrace death as a necessary part of the whole. Like the hero of the spiritual epic, they will be able to pass back and forth from time into eternity, in and out of the belly of the whale, endlessly and without harm to their soul. Like Ishmael on the masthead, when he loses all attachment to his ego, or on the third day of the chase, when he finally sees Moby Dick for the first time, breaching out of the water in an epiphany of beauty and power, they will find that the material world is not a "wall" of imprisonment but a door, or what Campbell calls a "Wall of Paradise," that opens to reveal the divinity behind all creation.[32] This door or Wall of Paradise is made up of the "coincidence of opposites," all the dyadic forces that define human experience in this world—life and death, land and sea, sickness and health, day and night, male and female, matter and spirit—the same conflicting forces that make up the subject of *Moby-Dick*. Those like Ahab, whose egotism leads them to see the world selfishly, defensively, will never be able to penetrate the wall, no matter how they strain or rage. Like the *Pequod*'s captain, who makes his last appearance bound, literally, to the "wall" of Moby Dick, they will die without knowing that their true selves forever lie waiting on the other side. Like Ahab, who insists on playing the game according to his own rules, they will never garner the victor's prize, never know the triumph that lies beyond life's tragedy.

III. THE FIRE SERMON

On the practical level, part three of *Moby-Dick* focuses on the difficulties of the hunt, on the pursuit, capture, killing, and dismembering of the whale. Opening with "The First Lowering," chapter 48, it runs through chapter 76, "The Battering-Ram," in which Ishmael describes the "dead, impregnable, uninjurable wall" of the whale protecting the buoyant "mass of tremendous life" that swims behind it (337). In other words, it stops just short of "The Great Heidelberg Tun" (chapter 77), in which Ishmael describes the initial step of the fourth stage, the breaking into the interior of the whale, the practical equivalent of the mythological journey down into its belly. Though the pursuit of the whale has a spiritual dimension, too, it is first and foremost a worldly, carnal business, a hunger of the flesh for the flesh.

Melville defines the hunt as a form of cannibalism, an instance of "the universal cannibalism of the sea" (274). It is but another name for the process of dismemberment encoded in the brutal notion of "eat or be eaten." In the "fiery hunt" for the albino whale, Ahab makes the appetite of the crew burn for satisfaction, as he himself burns for revenge (195). But the desires of the flesh are self-consuming; to heed them, as Ahab does in his mad chase after Moby Dick, leads to death, is itself a form of dying into death. In all the religious mythologies of the world, the way of all flesh is the way of fiery destruction. So too in *Moby-Dick*. What is required is a spiritual view of the hunt, such as Melville's narrator comes to have. But such a view can be achieved only after a rigorous purification, a cleansing of the senses in a trial by fire, such as Ishmael experiences momentarily at the end of "The First Lowering." Only then will the hero find his way to a face-to-face confrontation with the "image of the ungraspable phantom of life," the soul within himself that waits to sound its name.

In the journey of the hero, the third part of *Moby-Dick* corresponds with the crisis, what Campbell calls "the ultimate adventure," the meeting, and marriage, with the alluring figure known as the Queen Goddess of the World. In Melville's handling of this stage of the epic plot, the great whale is an instance of this queenly apparition. Appearing in the book for the first time in "The First Lowering" and "The Spirit Spout" (chapters 48 and 51), Moby Dick proves a tantalizing yet elusive lure. Moreover, there are other whales, lesser versions of the Queen, to be encountered before the "grand hooded phantom" (7) becomes the exclusive object of the *Pequod*'s hunt. In fact, in Melville's novel the crisis is an exceptionally protracted, on-again-off-again affair, stretching beyond the third and into the fourth and fifth parts of the narrative. While Moby Dick is not, of course, a ravishingly beautiful woman or goddess, it is androgynous and in other respects corresponds with the character of this mythical figure. Its "vast milky mass," we are told in "The Town-Ho's Story," has an "appalling beauty" (256); and while its power and aggressiveness are dominant, its conventional female character is evident in the fact that it lures the sailors on at the same time it runs away from them. More important than the whale's gender, however, is the fact that, like the goddess of myth and religion—like Beatrice or the Virgin Mary—the great whale is the embodiment of every perfection. By the simple fact of its mesmerizing power, it assures the soul that the bliss of memory, whether remembered from the womb or imagined as a lost ideal, will be ours once again.[33]

Even so, the Queen Goddess, whether remembered as one's mother or as the Mother Nature that nurtures us all, is a complex, even contradictory, figure. Like the whale, she is both benign and evil, sustaining and punishing, enticing and forbidding. She thus represents all existence, all knowledge, or all that can be known. The false hero, who sees with a fearful eye, will recognize only one dimension of her, as Ahab recognizes only the whale's malice. But the true hero will see and appreciate her totality, as Ishmael comes to see and appreciate the doubleness of the White Whale.

The tale of "The First Lowering," which opens part three, is a prophetic version of the ultimate adventure, an epitome of what the hero's coming home to God will entail and what it will require of him. At the same time, it dramatizes the relative spiritual development of each of the major characters and measures their readiness to meet the great God face to face. Although we are never actually told that the school of whales that prompts this first lowering includes Moby Dick, the idea is suggested symbolically that the one whale featured in this scene is an extraordinary, godlike beast very much like Moby Dick. One clue to Melville's intention is the seemingly innocuous chapter title, which refers not simply to the process of the men going over the side in their whaleboats prior to giving chase but to the scowling or "clouding over" of the face of the godhead whom they would capture. Certainly this pun is intended, for Melville later uses "lowering" with the very same meaning in describing the whale's mighty brow (346). Moreover, it should be noticed that the whale featured here comes and goes in a squall, which is itself preceded by a sudden clouding over. Indeed, the whale is saved by a squall that bursts on the whaleboats right at the instant when Queequeg darts his harpoon into it. For all its gritty realism, it is a moment much like the symbolic moment in *Walden,* when the loon Thoreau has been chasing across the Pond suddenly calls on the "god of loons" to whip up a wind to save him.

After the boats have been lowered, the whales all begin to dive under the surface. Their disappearance provides an opportunity for each of the main characters to strike a typical pose: Starbuck, for example, sits "silently eyeing the vast blue eye of the sea" in cool anticipation of their return; and Flask complains impatiently, "I can't see." It is the Indian, Tashtego, however, whose people were the first to try to interpret the whale's ways, who first spies the school again, though "no whale, nor any sign of a herring," as Ishmael says emphatically, would have been visible to a landsman (221–22).

By contrast, the oarsmen—and this includes Ishmael—are not permitted to see much of anything. With their backs toward the whale, they must "put out their eyes" and give every drop of energy to rowing (223). Like Melville's readers, they can experience the whale only secondhand, "with their eyes on the intense countenance of the mate in the stern of the boat," reading there their future. To be sure, all their other senses are alive to the "thrilling" experience of the imminent confrontation. To a man such as Ishmael, "who for the first time finds himself pulling into the charmed, churned circle of the hunted sperm whale," it is akin to a visionary experience, producing strange and powerful emotions, like the feelings of "the dead man's ghost encountering the first unknown phantom in the other world" (223–24). But, like any neophyte, he must be careful not to look on the face of the great god directly. For unless he is prepared for the revelation of its full magnificence, he will be overwhelmed; he will become a dead man's ghost in literal fact. As Flask explains, in the sperm-whale fishery it is an "unalterable law" that an oarsman must pull himself "back-foremost into death's jaws." "I should like to see a boat's crew backing water up to a whale face foremost," he exclaims, with more meaning than he knows. "Ha, ha! the whale would give them squint for squint, mind that!" (227). Significantly, Ishmael never sees a live whale, never sees one face to face, free of the distorting effect of the sea, until the very last chapter. There, in the culminating moment of his odyssey, as he watches from a distance, he finally sees Moby Dick breach out of the water in an epiphany of power and beauty, just before it destroys the *Pequod*.[34]

Throughout "The First Lowering," the *Pequod*'s encounter with the whale is described in religious terms. Most tellingly, after the whale escapes in the storm and the boat is wrecked, Ishmael speaks not just of their surviving a test but of their being transformed by it. In language that evokes a ritualistic trial by fire, he says that when the wind increased to a howl, "the whole squall roared, forked, and crackled around us like a white fire upon the prairie, in which, unconsumed, we were burning; immortal in these jaws of death!" (225). This pivotal chapter, then, ends early the next morning, with a stove boat and a rescue ship, in a curious foreshadowing of the final scene of the novel.

"The Hyena" (chapter 49), as its puzzling title implies, confirms that for Ishmael the experience described in "The First Lowering" was a profoundly transfiguring one. The "last man" to be dragged aboard the *Pequod* after the squall, Ishmael immediately shakes off his fear of these perilous events, just as he shakes off the water from his dunking. After confirming with his shipmates that the violence of their recent encounter is anything but a rarity in the sperm-whale fishery, he goes jauntily below deck to make out a draft of his will. In doing so, he shows his readiness, qualified though it may be (it is, after all, only a rough draft he writes), to give up his attachment to the things of this world and make peace with death, even if the best he can manage is a kind of perverse pleasure in the process. Pushed to the brink of disaster in the storm, he returns to the ship with a new outlook on life, a "free and easy sort of genial, desperado philosophy." Whereas previously he had looked on the prospect of his own death as "a thing most momentous," it now strikes him as simply part of the "vast practical joke" that defines the universal scheme of things. He may be able to see the humor of the joke only "dimly," but, as the title of this chapter suggests, if one is going to enter into "death's jaws" it is best to do so with the grin of the hyena on one's own countenance. For to adopt Ishmael's "genial, desperado philosophy" is to transcend the anguish at the prospect of dismemberment and death that so torments Ahab. It is to reach a state of mind where "nothing dispirits, and nothing seems worth while disputing." One simply "bolts down" everything, "all creeds, and beliefs . . . all hard things visible and invisible" as "an ostrich of potent digestion gobbles down bullets and gun flints"—in effect, "eating" any and all experience, even death, rather than being "eaten" by it (226–27).

While at first glance this seemingly cannibalistic philosophy may seem impious, it is actually based on an implicit faith in God and His wisdom, or so Ishmael suggests. Ishmael may regard the Creator as an "unseen and unaccountable old joker," bestowing such "jolly punches" as death and disaster on his helpless creatures, but Ishmael presumes nonetheless that He still exists, actively presiding over all creation. The problem is simply that man fails to comprehend His ways, fails to understand the nature of the "general joke" (226–27). With a faith, therefore, that everything that happens in this world has some mysterious purpose, Ishmael releases his hold on what few belongings he has (signing them over to Queequeg, his "legatee") and vows to take "a cool, collected dive at death and destruction." Having dispensed with his worldliness, and with it any concern for his ego, Ishmael then experiences an unexpected benefit: he suddenly feels as though "a stone was rolled away from my heart." Like Lazarus, who was lowered into his grave only to be resurrected again, Ishmael can say, "I survived myself; my death and burial were locked up in my chest," there to remain forever, in the keeping of his heart (227–28).

Having proved himself in "The First Lowering," then, Ishmael and the rest of the crew soon encounter a mysterious "silvery jet" that seems to lure them on. "Lit up by the moon, it looked celestial; seemed some plumed and glittering god uprising from the sea" (232). It is "The Spirit-Spout" of chapter 51; and while some of the sailors swear it is Moby Dick, Ishmael never does offer an opinion on the matter. Whatever its true identity, the appearance of the beckoning jet clearly advances the adventure of the hero to a new, and distinctly spiritual, stage. Significantly, when Fedallah cries out at seeing the spout, the crew responds not with terror but with "pleasure," and as Ishmael says, "almost every soul on board instinctively desired a lowering." All of them sense the White Whale to be the incarnation of the soul they all yearn to discover. At this point, even the *Pequod* seems to be propelled by a new impulse, one that runs counter to its regular movement in the mundane realm of the whaling business. When the unusual order is given to set all sails in pursuit of the strange spout, the ship is said to rush along "as if two antagonistic influences were struggling in her—one to mount direct to heaven, the other to drive yawingly to some horizontal goal." Still, like the Queen Goddess of the World, even the spirit-spout, for all its mighty allure, is a figure of "dread" as well as of pleasure—a thing of doubleness. Appearing sporadically but always at night thereafter, this "flitting apparition" generates great apprehension among the crew, "as if it were treacherously beckoning us on and on, in order that the monster might turn round upon us, and rend us at last in the remotest and most savage seas." Intuitively, these rude, superstitious sailors know they have a spiritual and an earthly nature, a soul and an ego, and that the life of the one is the death of the other. They know, instinctively, that they are akin to Ahab, the dying man of whom Ishmael observes, "on life and death this old man walked" (233).

In most of the remaining chapters of this third part of *Moby-Dick,* Ishmael turns his attention to an exploration of a very different sort of effort to capture the whale, one close to his own concerns as a writer. These chapters center on the wide variety of artistic attempts, by men working in diverse media, to picture the whale as they themselves, supposedly, have seen it. These include chapters 55–57—"Of the Monstrous Pictures of Whales," "Of the Less Erroneous Pictures of Whales," "Of Whales in Paint; in Teeth; &c."—as well as chapters 74–75, which depict the heads of the sperm and right whales. Less obviously, they also include the first three of the "gam" chapters, in which sailors from the *Albatross,* the *Town-Ho,* and the *Jeroboam* relate tales of their encounters with Moby Dick. And they include others as well, such as the chapter on "Brit," on "The Whale as a Dish," and "The Battering Ram." All in all, three-quarters of the chapters in this section concern portraits or representations of the whale, the notable exceptions being those that treat whaling instruments—"The Line," "The Dart," and "The Monkey-Rope"—particularly such instruments as are used to secure, or gain entrance into, the whale.

While the many portraits help generate the sense of variety and density that an epic treatment of the subject requires, they also serve to bring into relief Ishmael's fixation on the question of what distinguishes a true picture from a false one, a report of someone's experience of the genuine article from one that has been adulterated by subjective temperament or point of view. In a world of "fanatic" Shaker prophets like Gabriel (315) and "corrupt" Lima priests (249), of devil-worshiping Parsees and "insane old" whaling captains

(237), there is reason to doubt the testimony of those who claim to know what they have seen when they claim to have seen something as strange as a living whale, particularly a white whale.

What keeps Ishmael from presenting a slanted or distorted view of this creature is that his view is never so simpleminded, or so intractable, as to be unqualified. It is always provisional, the product of what he admits to be personal opinion and not what he claims to know with absolute certainty. Typically, his view is as free of egotism as is humanly possible, short of his reaching the "transparent eyeball" state of Pip, after the cabin boy has become a "castaway." Even though by the time he writes his tale Ishmael has become an experienced whaler, one who has served in "various whalemen of more than one nation" (288), he himself never presents a final, authorized view of the whale or its meaning. He knows how difficult it is to get a clear, unobstructed view of the thing itself in its living, moving form. Most often, all that anyone knows about the whale is derived from its skeleton or from a carcass stranded on shore, and these lifeless forms can hardly be said to give a true idea of the "noble animal itself in all its undashed pride." The living whale, "in his full majesty and significance, is only to be seen at sea in unfathomable waters," Ishmael explains, and even then one can rarely get a totally unobstructed view. Even if one were lucky enough to see a live whale up close and afloat, "the vast bulk of him is out of sight," obscured, even distorted, by the water around him. As for seeing a living whale out of the water, there are precious few opportunities, for "it is a thing eternally impossible for mortal man to hoist him bodily into the air, so as to preserve all his mighty swells and undulations" (263).

Even when it comes time for Ishmael, then, to paint "something like the true form of the whale as he actually appears to the eye of the whaleman," he makes no pretense of depicting a living whale. Instead, he restricts himself to the moment "when in his own absolute body the whale is moored alongside the whale-ship" (260). Because the chance of seeing a living whale out of the water is so slight, therefore, "the great Leviathan is that one creature in the world which must remain unpainted to the last." To the landsman especially, this is a matter of some consequence. For, without an accurate picture, "there is no earthly way of finding out precisely what the whale really looks like." The only alternative is to go to sea in search of the whale yourself. But then, as Ishmael observes, "you run no small risk of being eternally stove and sunk by him" (264). Much the same might be said of the would-be hero's difficulties in capturing a glimpse of the true nature of the self or soul. Either the ego obstructs any view of the soul or it imprisons it, as it does in Ahab's case. The potential hero thus fails to recognize the self for the Leviathan that it is and dies without experiencing any higher promise to life. If one undertakes the challenge of the journey on his own, he runs the risk of being destroyed or overwhelmed or of being driven cravenly back to land, none the wiser for the effort.

In "Stubb Kills a Whale," chapter 61, the *Pequod* encounters its second whale of the voyage and Ishmael sees a live whale partially out of the water for the first time, enough to get a view of its tail. This, then, continues a carefully developed pattern in the later sections of the book, whereby the whale is revealed to Ishmael in increments or stages. While the whalemen quietly draw nearer, the monster suddenly turns up flukes, flitting its tail "forty feet into the air, and then [sinking] out of sight like a tower swallowed up." Significantly, as one of three men then on the lookout, Ishmael takes part in the sighting of this whale, and he does so, almost paradoxically, while lost in a "spell of sleep" induced by an empty sea—when the unconscious can make contact with its objective correlative, the surrounding ocean. Slipping into a dreamy mood, not long before the sighting, Ishmael observes that "at last my soul went out of my body; though my body still continued to sway" (282). Then instantly, as he explains, using imagery that foreshadows his near-drowning at the end, "bubbles seemed bursting beneath my closed eyes; like vices my hands grasped the shrouds; some invisible, gracious agency preserved me; with a shock I came back to life." Miraculously, in one of the great moments in the novel, when Ishmael opens his eyes, the image that greets him is the image of this invisible, grace-filled, life-preserving agency of the leviathanic self, slightly submerged in the sea but alive and "lazily undulating." "And lo!" he exclaims, "close under our lee . . . a gigantic Sperm Whale lay rolling in the water . . . his broad, glossy back, of an Ethiopian hue, glistening in the sun's rays like a mirror" (283). Somehow it is as though it had always been there, but Ishmael's egoistic defenses had kept him from being aware of it. But now, in this strangely relaxed mood, what meets his startled gaze, as he opens his eyes, is the glistening mirrorlike surface of the whale, the image of his own ungraspable soul reflected back to him.

In contrast to the sublimity of the moment of Ishmael's waking to his first glimpse of a living sperm whale, the next scene, "Stubb's Supper," describing the bloody aftermath of the hunt, is a comic orgy of the senses. Once the beast has been slain, and the "inert, sluggish corpse" hauled back and secured to the ship, all high-mindedness disappears as Ahab and Starbuck make their exit, and the crude second mate, "flushed with conquest," prepares to enjoy a ceremonial steak from the victim's choicest part. Stubb is a "high liver," in the low, ironic sense of the phrase, for he is "somewhat intemperately fond of the whale as a flavorish thing to his palate" (291–92). Given that the whole of this scene, with the men on deck cutting into the steak and the sharks below feeding on the carcass, captures the central theme of what Melville calls "the horrible vulturism of earth" (308), it is fitting that Stubb should preside here. For as one who combines the fleshly appetites of Flask and the spiritual tendencies of Starbuck, he is just the one to call for the black cook to preach to the sharks and urge them to curb their rapaciousness.

Fleece's sermon is the central rhetorical statement in the third part of *Moby-Dick,* the centerpiece, in fact, of the whole novel. Though it verges on being a piece out of a vaudeville comedy routine, with Stubb as straight man, it has a serious undertone that reflects the entire rationale of the hero's struggle. In his sermon warning against the hungers of the flesh, the old black cook speaks a timeless wisdom. His words may fall on deaf ears, as Melville must have feared his whole narrative might, but Fleece has the right idea when he tries to take into account the fallen nature of his congregation and asks them not to change themselves beyond what is possible. Instead, he enjoins them to acknowledge their dual nature and to use the one side to control the other. "Your woraciousness, fellow-critters," he apostrophizes, "I don't blame ye so much for; dat is nature, and can't be helped; but to gobern dat wicked nature, dat is de pint. You is sharks, sartin; but if you gobern de shark in you, why den you be angel; for all angel is not'ing more dan de shark well goberned" (295).

Despite the simplicity of his appeal, however, Fleece knows his effort will prove futile. Creatures of appetite will not pay attention to good spiritual counsel "till dare bellies is full," and, as even Fleece understands, "dare bellies is bottomless" (295). Yet what neither he nor Stubb seems to realize is that there is but one alternative to a life of the flesh: as the second mate himself says, after he discovers that Fleece has overcooked his whalesteak, "You must go home and be born over again" (296). The way of the hero is the only way, the way of death and rebirth. Clearly this is what Melville meant when he has Stubb tell Fleece in his bantering way, just moments later, that he cannot expect to get to heaven "by crawling through the lubber's hole . . . no, no, cook, you don't get there, except you go the regular way, round by the rigging" (297).

Fleece's "fire sermon" is an epitome of the whole third part of *Moby-Dick,* which brings into sharp focus the author's fixation on the life of the flesh. "Stubb's Supper," "The Whale as a Dish," "The Shark Massacre," "Cutting In," "The Blanket," and "The Funeral" (chapters 64–69) together evidence a deep preoccupation with the body of the whale and its dismemberment. But the chapters also show an equal preoccupation with the body of man, with the pleasures and needs and sins of the flesh of humankind. In fact, Melville has constructed his story in such a way that practically everything about the whale is symbolic of some fundamental human trait or truth or provides an occasion for examining the parallel ways of humanity. In every detail, it is fraught with human meaning, and in this way, too, it is a profoundly epic work.

Though he claimed not to "oscillate in Emerson's rainbow," Melville agreed with Emerson's famous axiom that "the whole of nature is a metaphor of the human mind." At the time he wrote *Moby-Dick,* he too believed, as Emerson proclaimed in *Nature,* that "the laws of moral nature answer to those of matter as face to face in a glass."[35] The process of "cutting in," or stripping away the whale's flesh, for example, is to be understood as a metaphor for the process of fleshly discipline or self-denial that one must follow to attain spiritual well-being. Similarly, these several chapters, going back to "Stubb Kills a Whale," shadow forth the whole process of life's unfolding, from birth to death, as one of dismemberment and dying. While in the beginning Ishmael sees the whale's body as something holy, glistening in the sun, by the time it has been gouged and chewed by sharks, cut into by the crew and stripped of its "blanket," it lies at its funeral still colossal but "desecrated" (309).

However, as the novel's quintessential metaphor for the soul, the whale is more than a symbol. It is a paradigm of all human behavior, the ultimate guide or authority in the hero's journey to self-understanding. While earlier Ishmael had more than hinted that there is something valuable to be learned from the whale, it is not until the first of the anatomy chapters—particularly "The Blanket," together with "Cutting In"—that he makes explicit the idea that mankind should actually model itself after the whale. It is in this sense that the whale can be understood to embody, like the figure of the Goddess of the World, the totality of what can be known.

In the anatomy chapters such as these, the trials of the hero in his encounters with the whale can be seen to be educative, and his willingness to imperil his life in this bloody business can be seen to pay off handsomely. For it is, after all, only with the firsthand experience of whaling that one can gain the wisdom the whale has to offer. In chapter 68, after deciding that the whale's skin is constituted not of the thin isinglass substance at the outermost surface of the beast but of the whole enveloping layer of its blubber, Ishmael points out that this thick mass is like a "blanket or counterpane," an image that recalls the counterpane Ishmael had shared with Queequeg in the Spouter-Inn. Like that earlier counterpane, the whale's "blanket" permits its inhabitant "to keep himself comfortable" in any weather, in any climate. "Herein we see," Ishmael concludes, in a little "fire sermon" of his own, "the rare virtue of thick walls.... Oh, man! admire and model thyself after the whale! Do thou, too, remain warm among ice. Do thou, too, live in this world without being of it" (307).

In a similar fashion, later, when considering the sperm whale's head as it hangs from the side of the ship, Ishmael argues the wisdom of patterning the development of one's mind after the whale's. Hypothesizing that, with one eye on either side of its head, the whale must be able to "attentively examine two distinct prospects, one on one side of him, and the other in an exactly opposite direction" at the same time, Ishmael reasons that the brain of the whale must be "much more comprehensive, combining, and subtle than man's," not more capacious. "Why then do you try to 'enlarge' your mind?" he asks; and then, taking his cue from the example of the whale, he offers the simple injunction to "Subtilize it" instead (331). Given the fundamental doubleness of the world, its goodness and its evil, the ability to take in its contradictions simultaneously is more than an asset; it is a prerequisite to one's seeing it whole, as the hero must learn to do.

More than a subtle brain, however, or thick walls, what one needs in order to survive in this world of dangers, what one needs for the health of his or her soul, is a "battering ram" like the whale's, a mighty, unfeeling instrument for protecting the life force as one goes about one's business. As in other respects, so here, the sperm whale is a model of engineering mastery: simple in design, reliable in operation—above all, effective. Like an enormous forehead, but with padding twenty feet thick covering the cranium, the battering ram of the sperm whale lacks "a single organ or tender prominence of any sort whatsoever." Layered over with an envelope of "boneless toughness," it will resist the sharpest lance darted by the strongest arm. Yet it is more than a means of defense; as Ishmael's term for it suggests, it is intended to be used actively, aggressively, offensively, as a billy goat uses its horns to defeat a foe or clear a path to some goal. What makes this "dead, impregnable, uninjurable wall" so extraordinary, so formidable, Ishmael explains, is that it is "unerringly" impelled by "a mass of tremendous life, only to be adequately estimated as piled wood is—by the cord; and all obedient to one volition, as the smallest insect." With such an instrument, there is virtually nothing the whale's gigantic willpower cannot accomplish. For the whale, to "stove a passage through the Isthmus of Darien," and mix the Atlantic with the Pacific, would hardly be too tall an order (337–38).

Unfortunately, there is no equivalent of this battering ram in the human makeup (except, possibly, the relatively puny nose). However, the important thing is for Melville's readers to be able to believe in the irresistible power of the self that is the human equivalent of the mass of life behind the whale's forehead. For should they be able to do that, should they be able to believe that they have a similar forcefulness within themselves, it would be *as if* they had a battering ram just like the whale's, and they would then be able to venture out to confront the forbidding truth of human experience without being scared away or overwhelmed. "Unless you own the whale," Ishmael explains, unless you have witnessed his infinite power firsthand and believe in it for yourself, "you are but a provincial and sentimentalist in Truth." But because "clear Truth is a thing for salamander giants only to encounter," one must either *be* a whale, or be *like* a whale, not to be overcome when one confronts such Truth (338). Those who are "provincials"—that is, those who have not undertaken a journey such as Ishmael's—will have no chance of surviving such an encounter when it occurs, for they will lack the faith and self-confidence required to meet the truth of human limitation and mortality.

Speaking at this point as one who has completed the cycle of the hero's adventure and thus knows the Truth, Ishmael signals the end of the third part of *Moby-Dick* by putting to the reader an oracle's sort of question. Employing an image of the aspiring hero at the moment of crisis, he asks rhetorically, "What befel the weakling youth lifting the dread goddess's veil at Sais?" (338). It is a simple question, so simple that even those who do not know the story of the great Egyptian mother of the gods will sense Melville's meaning: it is the unseasoned "provincials" or unbelievers of the world who will lose out in the ultimate test. Lacking the talent, courage, or fortitude of the true hero, they will fail to win the boon of love, or charity, that Campbell defines as "life itself enjoyed as the encasement of eternity."[36] "The encasement of eternity" is an apt description of the central object in the next chapter, "The Great Heidelberg Tun," which begins the fourth part of the novel. For the great "tun" contains the highly prized spermaceti "in its absolutely pure, limpid, and odoriferous state," the "most precious" of all the whale's "oily vintages" (340).

IV. DEATH BY WATER

"The Great Heidelberg Tun" is an important threshold chapter, marking the beginning of the questers' descent into the whale. Having caught, killed, and dragged a sperm whale to the ship and then stripped away the blubber and beheaded it, the crew hoists the head against the *Pequod*'s side in preparation for the difficult maneuver of breaking into the interior case or "tun." Earlier, in chapters 74 and 75, Ishmael had imagined himself going inside the mouths of a sperm whale and a right whale while conducting a tour of the two as they hang on opposite sides of the ship. But chapter 77 signifies the first actual venture inside a whale, literally a cutting through the wall in search of buried treasure. When such efforts are successful, the end result is "the Baling of the Case," or retrieval of the precious "sperm," from the large reservoir within the whale's head (339).

In this and the following chapter, "Cistern and Buckets," where Queequeg rescues Tashtego from the whale's head after it breaks loose and starts sinking, Melville begins using language that involves a vast conceit whereby the sperm oil stands for the vital "fluid" of the human soul. Repeatedly described as "precious" or "invaluable" and "pure," the sperm is said to be contained in the "sanctuary," or "secret inner chamber and sanctum sanctorum," of the whale. This curiously holy, sexually charged, life-giving substance is Melville's version of the object of the epic quest in its most essential form, the "unalloyed" oil that requires a "marvellous," yet sometimes "fatal," operation to tap it, as Tashtego learns to his horror (339–40, 344). Not all whalemen, of course, succeed even at capturing the sperm whale, let alone at breaking into its tun and retrieving this most valued of prizes. Like the men of the *Virgin,* described in chapter 81, they may spend their days going from ship to ship begging a little oil, forever dependent on others for the light they need to show them the way.

The whole of part four of *Moby-Dick* focuses on the whale's interior. All the world seems rushing to gain entrance there, to search for its riches, to experience its transforming power, to *know* the beast from inside. Opening with Tashtego's accidental entombment in the sperm whale's tun, the fourth section closes with Ishmael's very deliberate venture inside a whale's skeleton, described in "A Bower in the Arsacides," where he has gone to gather measurements for his study of the magnitude of the monster (chapters 102–05). Along the way, Ishmael contemplates the "nut" or brain of the whale, which is buried deep in its head; he discusses the historical likelihood of Jonah's being swallowed into the whale's belly; he offers a chapter on "ambergris," the valuable, waxlike substance found deep in its bowels; and, in still more imaginative variations on this theme, he writes of his own experience of being encircled by a great swirling herd of whales in "The Grand Armada" and then of the ship's mincer encasing himself within the whale's foreskin in "The Cassock."

At least half of the chapters in part four are concerned with sundry methods for gaining access to the whale's interior and the various treasures to be retrieved there. Still other chapters elaborate on the central themes of part four by examining various containers for processing or holding the oil and other prizes once they have been collected from inside the whale. These include chapters on the hold of a whaleship, the *Jungfrau,* which is forever empty; on the hand, which breaks down lumps of spermaceti and ends by holding other hands; on the try-works," with its twin try-pots, each with a capacity for holding many barrels of oil; on the lamp; and the decanter. Even the chapter on "The Doubloon," a token containing real monetary value for the sailor who first sights Moby Dick, is related to the central theme of this section, as is the chapter on the story of Captain Boomer, of the *Samuel Enderby,* whose right arm was swallowed by the White Whale. Melville's preoccupation with the theme of containment in part four is symptomatic of his interest in the vitalizing boon or treasure, the thing contained that is the object of the hero's quest. But it is also symptomatic of his interest in the process of the hero's being contained or imprisoned, and tried and transformed, as Jonah was alleged to have been, inside the whale.

Throughout part four of the narrative, then, Melville develops themes of death and resurrection, of recovery and rebirth, of the awakening of the self to new life. In the early chapters of this section, Tashtego is miraculously delivered and reborn through the daring "obstetrics" of Queequeg, after the Indian has slipped into the Great Tun and been "coffined, hearsed, and tombed" there (344).[37] Almost a victim of drowning after the head of the whale that confines him rips free of the *Pequod* and sinks into the sea, Tashtego is the first of several characters who experience a kind of "death by water" and live to tell about it. Jonah, first of all, and then Pip, Captain Boomer, and Ishmael all come to know something of this remarkable, life-changing fate. There is a death by land that is the common death; it is the "living death" of those who never venture from shore. But there is also a death by water, which is initiated by an escape from convention and leads to a dying to the world, as in baptism. This death ends in resurrection or rebirth, or in a saving glimpse of the world beyond this one. However, as Pip's example testifies, unless the breakthrough occurs within the ritual of the hunt, the experience can be so overwhelming as to drive the would-be initiate "mad" (414). He may return from his journey a changed man, but he will lack the self-command, or the semblance of sanity, required to make himself understood by others.

In developing the themes of transformation, of the hero's dying and renewal, in this section, Melville continues with the "anatomy" of the whale he had begun earlier. However, in keeping with these themes, he emphasizes, throughout part four, the whale's masculinity and godlike power. If one is to perform the equivalent of miracles and raise the living from the dead, if one is to bring oneself to life as if after a long, long sleep, one must possess the strength and regenerative power that are exemplified in the whale. In "The Prairie," Ishmael sings praises to the "mighty," "sublime" character of the sperm whale's brow, gazing on which "you feel the Deity and the dread powers more forcibly than in beholding any other object in living nature" (346). In "The Nut" he stresses the whale's backbone and hump, "the organ of firmness or indomitableness" (350). And in "The Fountain," "A Squeeze of the Hand," and "The Cassock," he celebrates the procreative powers of the whale, its sexual potency. The one whale that the men of the *Pequod* hunt down in this section, moreover, is a male, "a huge, humped old bull," and they do so after winning a race against the crew of a rival ship called the *Virgin* (352). Most of the book's many instances of so-called "male humor," in fact, are to be found in this section, particularly in "Schools and Schoolmasters," "Fast-Fish and Loose-Fish," "Heads and Tails," "The Pequod Meets the Rose-Bud," and "Ambergris," among others.

Such varied and persistent efforts at suggesting the masculinity of the whale are crucial to Melville's development of the penultimate stage in the hero's adventure. This is the stage represented in traditional religions and mythic stories as the atonement with the Father. Although it is typically cast in confrontational terms, it invariably leads to a reconciliation between the hero and his progenitor or ruler, for the hero must come to recognize that he will never achieve atonement by aggression or simple force of will. The Father, the ruling force of the world, is simply too powerful to be overcome by such means. As in other spiritual epics, so here: atonement results from the hero's renunciation of his own egoistic preoccupations and from his absolute trust in the Father's mercy. Of course Ahab, the man with the mortally wounded ego, lacks such trust, while Ishmael eventually acquires it. Indeed, it is his trust, his faith in the spirit within him, that frees him from Ahab's vengeful search.

Few aspirants ever manage to achieve atonement. The Father admits into His order only those who have shown themselves worthy. For if He fails to prevent those who are not really prepared for the role of authority that awaits them, everything will run to chaos, as it does in the story of the "scaramouch" Gabriel, the crazy Shaker prophet who by fear and cunning manages to gain an upper hand over almost everyone on the *Jeroboam* (314). Ahab's destruction, and the chaos he brings to his crew because of his supreme selfishness, is a variation on this theme. Yet Ahab is only the most spectacular failure in the book, its central paradigm of the false aspirant. There are others, particularly in this fourth part of the narrative. The episode involving the eternally empty German whaleship called the *Virgin* symbolizes this theme. So, too, does the subsequent episode involving the *Rose-Bud,* whose captain is tricked into giving up the ambergris from a foul-smelling old whale carcass. Unlike Ahab, however, these captains are neophytes in the art of whaling; when asked about Moby Dick, neither one can say he has even heard of him before.

Not even all of the *Pequod*'s crew, however, successful though they are as a group, are deserving whalemen. When it is discovered, in the episode with the Germans, that the old whale they have captured is diseased, and blind and crippled as well, Flask shows a malignant side to his character when he deliberately pricks the ulceration on the animal's flank. Flask may be the one who brings in this catch, but his sadistic action taints the spirit of the hunt. Clearly, he is too self-indulgent to deserve his reward, and subsequent events mysteriously preclude him from enjoying it. Almost immediately afterward, the dead whale's body takes on water and starts to go down. Though the crew manages to secure the sinking whale to the ship's side, it threatens to capsize her; the fluke-chains have to be cut, and the corpse disappears, carrying with it "all its treasures unrifled" (358).

Whether because of lack of skill or a corrupt heart, many aspiring whalemen never reap the rewards of the hunt. They are a discredit to their calling and will never know the glory of atonement. But as Ishmael argues in "The Honor and Glory of Whaling" (chapter 82), there have been "many great demi-gods and heroes, prophets of all sorts," over the ages, who have brought great distinction to the whaling profession. They are bona fide heroes, and together they constitute an "emblazoned . . . fraternity" of God's chosen. An improbable collection, to be sure, including Perseus, St. George, Hercules, Jonah, Ishmael himself ("though but subordinately"), and even the Hindu god Vishnu, each qualifies as a "doer of rejoicing good deeds" (361–63). Perseus, especially, the founder of "our brotherhood," is famous for his chivalry. Free of such selfish motives as the Flasks and the Derick De Deers of the world demonstrate, the "gallant Perseus" took up the hunt in order to "succor the distressed" (361).

Even more revealing is the example of Vishnu, the "grandmaster" of the whalemen's order, whom Brahma, the "God of Gods," created to preside over the work of reforming the world after the great deluge. Buried in Melville's abbreviated one-paragraph recreation of this story is the whole cycle of the epic hero's task—the transforming journey that leads to the discovery of a life-saving, world-changing treasure: in order to recover the mystical books known as the Vedas, books that would one day assist him in refashioning the world, Vishnu became incarnate in a whale and, "sounding down in him to the uttermost depths, rescued the sacred volumes" from the bottom of the sea (363). As Vishnu's story exemplifies, the responsibility of even the most divine hero, once he has attained his full powers, is to serve the renovation of the world, not his own personal interests.

The hero who achieves atonement with the Father takes on all the power and responsibility of the Father. This is so because, as Vishnu's story also makes clear, he and the Father are one. The voyage of the hero is thus a passage from sonship to fatherhood, one in which the aspirant discovers that he is his own Father, capable of performing the very same kinds of miracles he had thought only the Father could accomplish. As Melville suggests in "Jonah Historically Regarded," what the members of the whalemen's fraternity all have in common, besides their utter selflessness, is their capacity to work apparent miracles. However, these are not the sort of miracles that the doubtful old Sag-Harbor man thinks of when he questions the possibility of Jonah's actually fitting down a whale's throat or surviving the action of its powerful stomach juices. Instead, these are what might be called miracles of metaphor, imaginative feats whereby the storyteller jolts his reader into a new understanding of things, a new relation to the truth. As his ironic tone implies, Melville did not share the belief of the simple Portuguese priest that the report of Jonah's traveling to Nineveh all the way around the horn of Africa in just three days, while installed inside the whale, was "a signal magnification of the general miracle." And neither did he believe, with the devoted Turks who built a mosque in Jonah's honor as a sign of their faith in his story, that their holy structure contained "a miraculous lamp that burnt without any oil" (366). His was not the faith of the literal-minded.

However, as a writer, and as a man of imagination, Melville did believe in the transforming power of the *story* of Jonah. He believed that even the skeptical reader could be made to feel the truth and force of the language of metaphor. Certainly as one who himself believed in the undying conscience of the fugitive Jonah in Mapple's sermon, Melville felt there was such a thing, metaphorically speaking, as a "miraculous lamp" that burns without oil (366). As he shows, furthermore, at the beginning of "Pitchpoling" (chapter 84), right after mentioning the miraculous lamp of the Turks, he believed that one could, with the help of the imagination, be made to see all language, all the world even, as perfectly plastic and capable of revealing a figurative truth. In this chapter describing one of the finest of all "the wondrous devices and dexterities" that a whaleman must learn to master, Melville performs something of a miracle himself by turning a simple whaleboat into a lamp of a very unusual kind. Needing a whale for his demonstration of the "fine manoeuvre with the lance called pitchpoling," Melville chose this moment to describe Queequeg's peculiar practice of "anointing" his boat with grease to make it slide through the water, "rubbing in the unctuousness" as one would rub a magic lamp. "He seemed," Ishmael observes, "to be working in obedience to some particular presentiment," and then adds that "Nor did it remain unwarranted by the event." For toward noon of that same day (when the sun, emblem of the Father of all the gods, would have been at its meridian), several whales were "raised," as one might be said to "raise" a host of powerful genii (367–78). To the literal-minded, Queequeg would appear to be a miracle worker in this scene. But to the mind attuned to metaphor, Queequeg is simply a man who is in touch with the rhythms of nature, or at one with the gods of the deep, even as he is "at one" with his Father on high.

"Pitchpoling" ends with a clean kill and another miracle. Stubb, a man whose "coolness and equanimity in the direst emergencies" make him a master of this art, readies himself in a ritualistic way; and then, "with a rapid, nameless impulse" arching the spearlike pitchpole the necessary distance, he hits the "life spot" of the whale. Immediately the whale "spouts red blood" instead of "sparkling water." But this transubstantiation is hardly the miracle it might have been if Stubb were a bona fide hero. Though he is the one who blurts out the clue as to what his own transformation would require when he shouts that "all fountains must run wine today," he exposes his spiritual unreadiness when he speaks his preference instead for "old Orleans whiskey, or old Ohio, or unspeakably old Monongahela." What he calls "the living stuff" is not, of course, an earthly liquor or "spirit" (367–68). It is not even the blood of the dying god, symbolically apt though that may be. Instead, as the next chapter, "The Fountain," reveals, this "living stuff," which is the very essence of life, is symbolized by the whale's spout or fountain, an image of the Father as the great fountainhead of life (369).

As the scientific rhetoric of "The Fountain" makes clear, however, Ishmael is not one to jump directly to any conclusions as to what the whale's spoutings "mean." As usual, his way is more roundabout, an exercise in anatomy that soon slips into intellectual high jinx, only to end abruptly when a fountain of intuition erupts within Ishmael himself. For him, the question of the exact nature of the whale's spout, whether "really water, or nothing but vapor," seems an insoluble mystery, and he goes on to worry the subject in typical fashion for several pages (370).

Only after Ishmael has laid bare all the difficulties of deciding, and tried out several hypotheses, does he come to the conclusion that the whale's fountain is nothing but "mist" or "vapor." Though his reasoning is circular, and otherwise riddled with logical fallacies, his conclusion is perfectly sound. For it comes to him from one of those "intuitions of some things heavenly," as he says, in which he has come to have faith. It is an expression of the peculiar life-giving fountain that wells within every living thing (373–74). The essence of life, this marvelously inventive chapter demonstrates, is neither water nor air, and it is not some cunning mixture of the two called "mist." Rather, it is what Ishmael shows it to be at the end of his discourse, one of those "divine intuitions" that now and then shoot "through all the thick mists of the dim doubts in my mind," as they rise out of the unconscious into his consciousness—intimations of immortality as they make themselves known to the mortal side of his being.

Ishmael experiences this particular intuition, it should be emphasized, while looking at his own image in a mirror and watching a steamy vapor rise from his head, a little experiment he says he once conducted while in the midst of composing "a little treatise on Eternity," presumably *Moby-Dick* itself (374).

"Divine intuitions" of the truth—snatches, glimpses—these are some of the treasures that can come to the successful adventurer. They help clarify his perceptions; as Ishmael says, his "fog" is enkindled with a "heavenly ray" (374). But for the most part, mankind is cut off from the source of all truth, the Father. Trapped in their own consciousness, enslaved by their ego, people have no memory of God and no capacity for seeing Him in the present, no capacity for wonder and worship. In what Melville, in "The Prairie" (chapter 79), called "the now egotistical sky" of his own century, there is no evidence of the "gods of old." They all seem to have vanished, to be lured back again only by a "highly cultured, poetical nation," such as he himself was trying to inspire in writing *Moby-Dick* (347).

But as Ishmael says in this chapter that focuses on the expansive forehead of the whale, the image of God *can* be recollected, or restored to one, in the "imposing" frontal view of the sperm whale's head. The "high and mighty god-like dignity inherent in the brow" of any number of other creatures is so greatly amplified in the brow of the sperm whale that "gazing on it, in that full front view, you feel the Deity and the dread powers more forcibly than in beholding any other object in living nature." Unfortunately, however, to gain this "sublime" view, one has to place himself in the monster's charging path (346). And even then, one can at best only snatch a glimpse of it, for everyone but the most experienced whalemen—the harpooner and the mate—must actually face backward through all but the very last stages of any encounter with the whale.

Seeing the Father face to face represents the ultimate revelation in the hero's journey toward self-understanding, the supreme test of his readiness and character. Luckily, as we learn in "The Tail" (chapter 86), there are other views of the whale that are almost as inspiring of religious feeling, without being nearly so perilous as the front view. These, too, can have the effect of transforming the aspirant, as Ishmael's sight of the peaking of the whale's flukes transforms him, making him eager to "celebrate" the whale's tail, though it remains shrouded in mystery (375). "Excepting the sublime *breach*," he asserts, the peaking of the whale's flukes "is perhaps the grandest sight to be seen in all animated nature. Out of the bottomless profundities the gigantic tail seems spasmodically snatching at the highest heaven" (378).

Yet as important as this feeling of spiritual excitement, which the sight of the whale's upturned flukes can inspire, is the attitude of reverence for the

Most High that the poised tail itself seems to exemplify. Describing a remarkable scene he once witnessed while standing on the lookout one sunrise, Ishmael testifies that "I once saw a large herd of whales in the east, all heading towards the sun, and for a moment vibrating in concert with peaked flukes. As it seemed to me at the time, such a grand embodiment of adoration of the gods was never beheld, even in Persia, the home of the fire worshippers." He comes away from the experience with the idea that the whale is "the most devout of all beings," and in doing so he identifies yet another reason why all people should model themselves after this remarkable creature (378).

To be sure, there are some gestures of the tail that "remain wholly inexplicable" to Ishmael and certain other motions of its body that are "unaccountable" even to the most experienced hunter. As much as anything, the featureless face of the beast puzzles him even beyond the last act of his story. However, as is suggested by the biblical language he invokes, particularly from Exodus 33:23, Ishmael has come to believe in the whale as one is sometimes said to believe in a religion, in spite of his great ignorance of it. Thus chapter 86 ends with his confession that "The more I consider this mighty tail, the more do I deplore my inability to express it. . . . But if I know not even the tail of this whale, how understand his head? much more, how comprehend his face, when face he has none? Thou shalt see my back parts, my tail, he seems to say, but my face shall not be seen" (378–79).

In the next chapter, however, Ishmael launches into a broad if indirect series of hints as to the mysterious character of the whale's face, Melville's symbol for the inexpressible face of God. "The Grand Armada" is the centerpiece of the fourth part of *Moby-Dick;* it tells the story, first on a grand scale and then in miniature, of the whole epic hunt. What it reveals about the countenance of the whale—here imaginatively portrayed as the collective expression of a whole herd of whales viewed in close proximity to Ishmael's boat—is its moodiness or doubleness, its capacity to be both excited and calm, even at the same time. Ishmael opens the chapter at the moment when the *Pequod* is making its way through the Straits of Sunda into the China seas, the favored haunt of the White Whale. Passing through these straits, Ishmael says, one has the sense of entering "the central gateway opening into some vast walled empire"—the fabled East, with its "inexhaustible wealth of spices, and silks, and jewels, and gold, and ivory" (381). It is, of course, remindful of the hero's passage through the "wall" of the whale en route to the treasure. But the wealth that awaits the crew of the *Pequod* at this point is not a material kind of treasure, such as the Orient offers; it is instead "a spectacle of singular magnificence"—a great "host of vapory spouts" all spread across half the horizon "up-playing and sparkling in the noon-day air" (382).

Following a hard and lengthy chase in which the crew is made to earn its reward, they suddenly catch up to the whole herd of gallied whales, now seemingly "going mad with consternation." After Queequeg harpoons a lone whale on the edge of the caravan, the wounded beast, Ishmael says, threw "blinding spray in our faces, and then running away with us like light, steered straight for the heart of the herd" (385). Their external eyes thus blinded, the crewmen must instead trust their inner eyes, and what they see approximates a miraculous vision. As they are dragged deeper and deeper into the "frantic shoal," they come upon a great calm or "sleek," generated by the moisture even a quiet whale throws off, at the "innermost heart" of the immense herd. "Yes, we were now in that enchanted calm which they say lurks at the heart of every commotion" (385–87). Within moments, these simple whalemen have experienced the two sides of the Spirit of God that in the opening of Genesis is said to move over the face of the waters.

Now hemmed in by the "living wall" that shuts out all but the most courageous, skillful whalemen (the wall, Ishmael observes, "that had only admitted us in order to shut us up"), they are "visited by small tame cows and calves; the women and children of this routed host" (387). There in this magic circle, inside not a single whale but a whole pod of them, they witness leviathan versions of the same domestic rites of the bridal chamber and nursery that they had left behind on land. There they see images of creation, age-old images out of Genesis—the swelling forms of expectant mother whales and the motionless forms of nursing mothers; even a newborn, recently confined in its mother's belly, the "umbilical cord of Madame Leviathan" still joining them. "Some of the subtlest secrets of the seas," Ishmael exclaims, "seemed divulged to us in this enchanted pond. We saw young Leviathan amours in the deep" (388). Finally, Ishmael suggests that, in viewing this scene, he discovers what the successful hero always finds: the face of the Father and the face of the hero are one and the same.

In a single paragraph Melville captures the whole essence of the epic hunt when he has Ishmael give voice to the feeling of profound happiness that comes to him as he gazes into the enchanted pond at the center of this "grand armada":

> And thus, though surrounded by circle upon circle of consternations and affrights, did these inscrutable creatures at the centre freely and fearlessly indulge in all peaceful concernments; yea, serenely revelled in dalliance and delight. But even so, amid the tornadoed Atlantic of my being, do I myself still for ever centrally disport in mute calm; and while ponderous

planets of unwaning woe revolve round me, deep down and deep inland there I still bathe me in eternal mildness of joy. (388–89)

Saying this, Ishmael thus announces that he has at last looked into the same waters in which the young Narcissus had drowned—looked and seen and grasped the "ungraspable phantom of life" and discovered there an image not of wrath but of "eternal mildness of joy."

What it would be like to see the face of God, not as it is reflected in the image of the whale, but directly, is the solemn subject of "The Castaway" (chapter 93). Pip, the black cabin boy who is the central figure in this scene, is not a whaleman but a "ship-keeper," a role reserved for those having little or no standing as sailors (411). At a time of emergency, therefore, when he is rushed into service in one of the boats, he has no experience in the hunt and loses his head at the first moment of contact with the beast. When he leaps from the boat the first time, Stubb takes pity on him and acts immediately, "for God's sake," to save him. However, when he jumps a second time, the cabin boy is left behind on the open sea "like a hurried traveller's trunk," a fore-image of the box that will buoy up Ishmael in the end. Pip turns his face, in an attitude of dumb worship, "out from the centre of the sea" toward the sun, portrayed here as "another lonely castaway, though the loftiest and the brightest" (413). He is therefore one who looks at God face to face, without first going through the whaling ritual. The "awful lonesomeness" of being on an open ocean, Ishmael exclaims, "is intolerable. The intense concentration of self in the middle of such a heartless immensity, my God! who can tell it?" (414).

Having to take the full force of the light of the deity directly, without a medium to mute or channel it, Pip is simply overwhelmed. His earthly personality is destroyed. After a time, his "ringed horizon began to expand around him miserably" until the whole world and his own consciousness became one. In effect, he has opened his soul beyond the initial terror of meeting the Father and, in doing so, come to understand the beginning and the end of all creation. He and the great Father are thus reconciled. But from the hour of his rescue, Ishmael explains,

> the little negro went about the deck an idiot; such, at least, they said he was. The sea had jeeringly kept his finite body up, but drowned the infinite of his soul. Not drowned entirely, though. Rather carried down alive to wondrous depths, where strange shapes of the unwarped primal world glided to and fro before his passive eyes; and the miser-merman, Wisdom,

> revealed his hoarded heaps; and among the joyous, heartless, ever-juvenile eternities, Pip saw the multitudinous, God-omnipresent, coral insects, that out of the firmament of waters heaved the colossal orbs. He saw God's foot upon the treadle of the loom, and spoke it; and therefore his shipmates called him mad (414).

More than any other character in the book, Pip knows that the soul and God are one. Though his ego has been blasted, and with it his capacity for translating all he has witnessed, he alone among the crew has dived so deep as to sound the self to its bottom. He alone knows that, in the end, there is no death; there is really only life. Whether we recognize it or not, whether we will it or not, "we are all," as Ishmael says before Pip leaps a second time from Stubb's whaleboat, "in the hands of the Gods" (413).

Although "A Squeeze of the Hand," the next chapter, is radically different in tone from "The Castaway"—gentle and dreamy where the latter is grave and mystical—it should be read as a companion piece, for it confirms that the hand of the Father that holds us, though it may treat us with wrath, is ultimately a hand of forgiveness, mercy, and love. Whether it chastizes or comforts, it is a hand of support, one that acts out of concern for our best interests, like the so-called "supernatural hand" that the young Ishmael once woke to find holding his own hand hours after he had been sent to bed for some youthful misdeed (26). On the face of it, "A Squeeze of the Hand" concerns Ishmael's mollifying experience of squeezing lumps of spermaceti back into fluid form, the "hand" of the title, in this case, referring simply to the hand of Ishmael and of his respective co-laborers. For Ishmael it is a crucial, transforming experience, a pivotal event in his epic journey, for it results in his decision to break free of Ahab's magnetic hold. However, as an extended trope or pun on life-giving male sperm, "A Squeeze of the Hand" also celebrates the endless flowing of the seminal waters of the Creator, the "living stuff," to borrow Stubb's term, that jets from the eternal fountain to bring forth life out of nothingness.[38]

The hand of the Father that clenches in anger to chastise the child can also "squeeze" with a gentle firmness to give reassurance of His love, or it can open wide to release the treasure that promises the renewal of life. Significantly, Ishmael loses his ego, in this chapter, as well as his sanity, as Pip does in "The Castaway." "I squeezed that sperm," Ishmael exclaims, "till I myself almost melted into it; I squeezed that sperm till a strange sort of insanity came over me." But his transformation has not incapacitated him, as Pip's had incapacitated Pip. Instead, his experience of squeezing case has given birth to an almost mystical illumination that makes him value the common life as never before. This, then, is the greatest boon of all—not simply the "abounding, affectionate, friendly, loving feeling" Ishmael suddenly feels toward his fellow sailors, but the radically enhanced appreciation he feels for the life he had left behind on shore. "I have perceived," he concludes meditatively, "that in all cases man must eventually lower, or at least shift, his conceit of attainable felicity; not placing it anywhere in the intellect or the fancy; but in the wife, the heart, the bed, the table, the saddle, the fire-side, the country; now that I have perceived all this, I am ready to squeeze case eternally" (416). Yet as Ishmael's own example suggests, one cannot achieve the frame of mind required to appreciate such domestic pleasures, without first leaving the land and going to sea. What is more, unless he engages in the entire ritual of the hunt, the would-be hero will never be able to return home. If, like Pip, he happens on a shortcut to revelation, it will catch him unawares, and he will never be able to recover from the shock of recognition.

After "A Squeeze of the Hand" comes another notorious phallic chapter, "The Cassock," this one treating circumcision. But like its predecessor, "The Cassock" is more than a crude male joke. As Melville's use of religious imagery implies, the outlandish scene described here has thematic significance that links it with the most fundamental purposes of the hero's epic adventure. Chapter 95 sketches the process of the mincer's stripping, refashioning, and donning of the whale's foreskin in preparation for the task of chopping up the blubber to be "tried out" in the pots, much as a priest might be said to don his cassock in preparation for his performance of some holy office. The ritelike quality of these operations emphasizes that the whole process of breaking down the whale's blubber into precious oil, described in the next chapter, "The Try-Works," is a very serious affair indeed, the whalers' equivalent of the ritualistic dismemberment and sacrifice of harvest gods like Osiris to ensure the renewed life of the tribe in spring.

The process portrayed in "The Cassock" is, of course, a form of phallic worship, an ancient and widespread celebration of life that Melville alludes to in referring to the story of Queen Maachah in 1 Kings 15. When the circumciser cuts away the male's foreskin, he removes the protective cover of the phallus, thus exposing the symbol of life itself; that is the chief purpose of the rite. But in this scene from *Moby-Dick,* when the mincer substitutes himself for the phallus by slipping inside its cover, Melville thus symbolizes that man is the source of his own life, that he can attain the state of immortality only by becoming so *like* the whale as to put himself in its place, inside the walls of its magically insulating skin. This "investiture alone," Ishmael says of the foreskin, "will adequately protect him" (420). Without it, the mincer runs the risk of self-mutilation, of dismembering his own toes and more, as Ahab may be said to do. In this respect, the symbol of the cassock also serves to inform the meaning of all the other protective coverings encountered earlier in the narrative—the counterpane, Mapple's raincoat, the nightgown, Queequeg's poncho, the whale's blanket—all the magic walls and covers that shield what Ishmael early in his story calls the "warm spark" of life from the threat of death (54).

As much as anything, "The Cassock" underscores the need for the protecting rituals of the whale hunt if one is to survive the final stages of the encounter with the Father. At the same time, however, "The Cassock" also captures the Oedipal nature of the human struggle with the Father for domination of the world. In Melville's rendering of this ageless conflict, it is not the initiates who are circumcised, as is usually the case, but the gods themselves, the whales. For in this way the whalemen signify their success at conquering the beast as well as their own fitness for enjoying the fruits of the hunt.

In turn, the whales sometimes appear to conspire with their pursuers, permitting themselves to be captured and sacrificed for the good of the whalemen, as when they become mysteriously "gallied" and suddenly stop, in the chase described in "The Grand Armada," at the very moment when their escape seems assured. So, too, in some early tribes, the elders are known to have sacrificed or bled themselves to supply sustenance for the young during the long period of their initiation. Such self-sacrifice reveals that the transfer of power is to be considered an impersonal process, one designed to guarantee the continued existence of the whole tribe, not that of any particular member or group. Only the fearful, the selfish, or the narcissistic, those who refuse the call to adventure, come in the end to know the gods by their fury rather than by their mercy. Like Ahab, whose severed leg constitutes a mitigated castration, their manhood is constantly threatened in the struggle with the powers that rule the self and the world. Instead of gaining strength or vitality over time, they seem, ineluctably, to be always losing what little life remains to them.

"The Try-Works" stands as the culmination of the process of breaking down the whale's flesh into light-bringing, life-giving oil, the final step in the transfer of power that will eventually result in the initiate's triumph over darkness, temporality, and death. Appropriately, the scene described here is also the turning point in Ishmael's quest for spiritual health, the moment of crisis when he comes to understand, more emphatically than he ever could have before, why he must renounce his part in Ahab's mad plan. The trying out of the whale's blubber is a fiery process comparable to the trying out or testing of the soul of the epic hero. It is an epitome of every man's life. Fittingly, it occurs in a place of special knowledge, the try-pots, where secrets are exchanged among the sailors and where Ishmael discovers a remarkable law of geometry. When the trying-out is allowed to go to completion, a wonderful transformation occurs.

All the impurities are burned off in a "horrible" smoke, leaving a fresh, sweet oil that only whalemen can know in its "unvitiated state" (422, 426).

When Ishmael first describes the operation, it is night, and the only illumination is provided by the hellish flame consuming the flesh of the whale "martyr" (422). Standing duty at the helm, he watches the harpooneers wildly gesticulating with their "huge pronged forks and dippers" as they alternately stoke the pots and stir up the fire. "Wrapped, for that interval, in darkness myself," Ishmael says, he achieves a state of mental clarity whereby "I but the better saw the redness, the madness, the ghastliness of others." In this grim mood, he thus finally penetrates the deeper significance of the scene, observing that "the rushing Pequod, freighted with savages, and laden with fire, and burning a corpse, and plunging into that blackness of darkness, seemed the material counterpart of her monomaniac commander's soul" (423).

After a while, however, Ishmael grows drowsy and loses this mental clarity, until finally the sight of the "fiend shapes" silhouetted against the fire "begat kindred visions in my soul." Under their influence, the influence of sleep, of death, he gets completely turned around and brings the ship to the verge of destruction before suddenly recovering his senses. "Starting from a brief standing sleep," he says, in language that describes also the mesmerizing influence of Ahab, "I was horribly conscious of something fatally wrong" (423). Sensing that the whole ship is headed in the wrong direction and will be destroyed, he wakes with a "stark, bewildered feeling, as of death" coming over him. Having righted the ship, and relieved to find that his "unnatural hallucination of the night" is over, he comes to recognize that, like Ahab, he had been looking "too long in the face of the fire," had in fact become "inverted," and "deadened," by it. "Turn not thy back on the compass," he then sermonizes, anticipating the time when Ahab will do just that; "accept the first hint of the hitching tiller; believe not the artificial fire, when its redness makes all things look ghastly. Tomorrow, in the natural sun, the skies will be bright; those who glared like devils in the forking flames, the morn will show in far other, at least gentler, relief; the glorious, golden, glad sun, the only true lamp—all others but liars!" (424–25).

Again, it is the sun, timeless image of the Father, that is the true guide to life. However, the sun is not simply a thing of glory and gladness in Melville's scheme. As an image of the Godhead, it is contradictory, double, a maddening mystery. Ruler of the known world, of all life, during the daylight hours, it is also lord of the underworld, of the dead, at night. But even during its ascendancy, the sun is bipolar, revealing a world of joy and pain, of benefit as well as loss. As Ishmael observes in a memorable apostrophe, "the sun hides not Virginia's Dismal Swamp, nor Rome's accursed Campagna, nor wide Sahara. . . .

The sun hides not the ocean, which is the dark side of this earth, and which is two thirds of this earth. So therefore, that man who hath more of joy than sorrow in him, that mortal man cannot be true—not true, or undeveloped." Conversely, the man who dwells only on the sorrows of life will become, in wise Solomon's phrase, one of the "congregation of the dead" even while living. Like Ahab, he will spurn the sun and worship instead the "artificial fire," the diminished, refracted, earthly form of the same vital energy that pours forth from the great source of all light and life (424–25).

As the potential hero of Melville's epic, then, Ishmael must learn to recognize the Father by His absence as well as by His glorious presence. In contrast to Starbuck, who professes in the doubloon scene not to believe in the sun at midnight, he must learn to have faith during the dark times of trial as well as during the periods of light. And he must come to see that the two are but parts of a single whole. The god of the sundoor, as Campbell says, is "the fountainhead of all the pairs of opposites." "In him are contained and from him proceed the contradictions, good and evil, death and life, pain and pleasure, boons and deprivation."[39] To the person who comes to understand this complexity, life is no longer a trial but a blessing. If, like the whaleman, he stays his course and seeks only what Ishmael, in "The Lamp" (chapter 97), calls "the food of light," he will meet such success as to "live in light" day and night, such an abundance of oil will be given to him. The light-giving, life-nurturing whale oil will permit him, even while asleep at night in his bunk, to be housed as in "some illuminated shrine of canonized kings and counsellors" (426). For Ishmael, then, this is the be all and end all of the whole whaling adventure: to live in light.

Given its proximity to Ishmael's discussion of the sun as "the only true lamp" at the end of chapter 96, the next chapter, "The Lamp," clearly correlates the light from the sun with the light from the oil of the sperm whale. These images in turn are related to the light that pours forth from the soul, as suggested first in Father Mapple's sermon, where the lamp hanging in Jonah's ship-cabin symbolizes the future prophet's conscience, the inner source of illumination available to all. *This* is the ultimate boon, the discovery that the light of the soul, of truth and immortality, is within oneself, that the hero and the Father are one. Sun, whale oil, soul, and God—all are variations of the same principle of light and life.

By contrast, the doubloon, a graven image of the sun, and the subject of the following chapter, is a false version of the guiding light. A circle of gold that Ahab has affixed high on the mainmast as a reward for the first sailor who sights Moby Dick, the doubloon competes with the sun for the crew's attention and homage. Indeed, it distracts them from the golden globe that the

Creator, in like manner, has set in the heavens to guide all humanity. Rather than generating light, however, the doubloon only reflects it, whatever the source, true or false. It is a mirror and not a lamp, to appropriate M. H. Abrams's well-known terms.[40] As each of the would-be communicants from among the *Pequod*'s crew makes his entrance to gaze on the gold coin, we are shown that the doubloon simply reflects back the subjective outlook of the observer. Leading off the procession, Ahab reveals his own egotism, and that of all the other observers as well, when he says, "There's something ever egotistical in mountain-tops and towers, and all other grand and lofty things; look here,—three peaks as proud as Lucifer" (431).

Still, the doubloon is a double thing—complex, contradictory, elusive in meaning. As the White Whale's "talisman," the doubloon is potentially more than a distraction from the true light. It is also a magical vehicle for raising Moby Dick, a mystical means of achieving the highest form of spiritual illumination. Minted in Ecuador, a country named for the region of the earth closest to the sun, and bearing in its inscription a segment of the zodiac with the "keystone sun" entering Libra, or the scales (the sign of judgment), the gold coin is presented as having powerful affinities with the sun. It is what Ishmael terms a "medal of the sun," or what Ahab calls a "coined sun," and it thus represents the ultimate source of all life (431).

Surely this is what Pip means when he refers to the doubloon as the "ship's navel," a common mythological image of the magical spot or "door" through which the vivifying energies of the spirit life pour into the world. The last to make his entrance in this scene, Pip offers no reading of the coin. Instead he articulates the unconscious motives, the propelling hunger of the *Pequod*'s whole crew, when he observes that the men "are all on fire to unscrew it" (435); all those who come forward to gaze on the doubloon want more than its monetary value as their reward for sighting Moby Dick. Their need is such that all of them, whether they know it or not, yearn to set free the flow of life into the body of the world, to restore vitality and meaning to their lives.

For Ishmael, Melville's single epic hero, this will be the life-saving consequence of his finally gaining a complete and unobstructed view of Moby Dick on the last day of the chase. All the power in the navel of the world, in the whale, will pour into him in the end in the form of spiritual energy or grace and buoy him up in the face of death. For, beneath the spot represented as the navel of the world, as Campbell explains this universal image, is "the earth-supporting head of the cosmic serpent, the dragon, symbolical of the waters of the abyss, which are the divine life-creative energy and substance of the demiurge, the world-generative aspect of immortal being."[41] As the successful hero, then, Ishmael is himself the umbilical point through which life's sustaining energies enter into the creation. To be sure, the doubloon is in fact nothing more than a gold coin; in Melville's scheme, it has no special, magical power. But as a symbol, it reveals that anything in the world, no matter how small or insignificant it might seem, is potentially divine. If one but knows how to tap it, and can let go of his ego, he will find that any point in the world is capable of becoming the place of special knowledge and power. For, to the true hero, the life force is everywhere.

Ishmael offers no reading of the doubloon. Like Pip, he has none of the ego involvement in the quest that keeps the other characters from seeing the coin objectively. Unlike the others, he has no selfish motive, nothing beyond simple curiosity, for continuing with the hunt at this point—nothing to prove, as Ahab tries to prove his indomitableness; nothing to gain, as Stubb and Flask think of gaining worldly riches; nothing to protect, as Starbuck tries to salvage his faith in a benevolent God. For Ishmael, the quest is all but over. Having sounded his soul, he has learned to master his ego and thereby achieved mastery of life. As he demonstrates in "A Bower in the Arsacides," where he speaks of making a visit, sometime later in life, to a temple formed of the skeleton of a great sperm whale on an imaginary island, Ishmael is able, finally, to go in and out of the "belly of the whale" without fear or harm, more or less at will. After he has once seen Moby Dick, he will have gone beyond the terrors of meeting the self that the whale signifies and will then understand the interior of the whale to be a holy, life-renewing place, a Chapel Perilous without perils.

It is true that "A Bower in the Arsacides" is the one episode in the book where Ishmael portrays himself as accomplishing the extraordinary feat of entering the whale's "belly." However, the ease with which he breaks through the wall of the ribs, as he says, and makes his winding way into the sanctum sanctorum of the beast and out again, suggests that he could do it again any time he wishes. So, too, of course, can anyone else, so easy is the hero's task, as long as one has the wisdom to do as Ishmael had done in following the example of Theseus, the ancient hero who used a simple string to find his way out of the Cretan labyrinth after venturing inside to kill the Minotaur. Using a "ball of Arsacidean twine" (is this, perhaps, the very same "ball of free will" that had dropped from his hand at the end of "The Mat-Maker"?), Ishmael says he wandered throughout the convoluted interior of the skeleton until his line ran out, and then he retraced his steps (450).

Like any successful epic hero, what Ishmael confronts, in the course of his descent, is his own mortality, the naked fact of death. Emerging from the same opening where he had entered, he says simply, "I saw no living thing within; naught was there but bones" (450). There is wry humor here, to be sure, and irony as well. But the fact remains that, in the metaphoric sense of the phrase, Ishmael has reached the end of the line. His quest is virtually finished; all that remains is for him to see Moby Dick, to glimpse a vision of God, and then make his return. By this point, he has defeated the hypos that originally sent him to sea; he has seen beyond his own death and is now prepared to do something worthy with the life that is left to him.

Like every epic hero once he has come to his journey's end, Ishmael possesses the power to save others, to guide the chosen few along the path of trials to the same life-transforming spot where he achieved his greatest triumph, the triumph of life over death. And indeed this is what he does, or tries to do. For, at the end of "The Fossil Whale" (chapter 104), Ishmael leads his reader into still another such holy place, a Barbary temple made of whale bones. It is said not only that a prophet who prophesied of Mahomet came from this spot but also that "the Prophet Jonas was cast forth by the Whale at the Base of the Temple" there. Whether coming to it or going away, one will forever find the belly of the whale to be a place of the highest spiritual power. A prophet himself in the end, Ishmael thus awaits the time when his reader, too, will issue forth a prophet of the soul. "In this Afric Temple of the Whale I leave you, reader," he says at the end of this chapter, "and if you be a Nantucketer, and a whaleman, you will silently worship there" (458). Future generations of readers can be assured that they, too, will benefit from Ishmael's example. In "Does the Whale's Magnitude Diminish?—Will He Perish?" the final chapter of the fourth section of *Moby-Dick,* Ishmael testifies that the whale grows larger, more powerful with every generation, that it is immortal in species, though individual bodies die. Clearly, what he says of the whale as a species he, and Melville, too, felt to be true of the human soul as well.

V. WHAT THE THUNDER SAID

Part five belongs to Ahab, the wounded king, or "grand, ungodly, god-like man" whose face bears a savage scar like the mark made by a lightning bolt (79, 123). In the last thirty chapters, he takes over center stage as Ishmael had in part one. Chapter 106, "Ahab's Leg," marks the transition into this final section. Here Melville's attention shifts sharply but deftly from the matter of Ishmael's growing independence and spiritual development to Ahab's earlier dismemberment by the White Whale, the event that precipitated the quest, and his inconsolable grief at his loss.

The previous chapter, "Does the Whale's Magnitude Diminish?—Will He Perish?" had made a firm case for the whale's immortality and thus for its appropriateness as a symbol for the soul. But "Ahab's Leg" comes as an immediate reminder of mankind's unalterable mortality, and of the inadequacy of pride or ego as a foundation or "standpoint." As Thomas Greene has argued, the epic hero must in the end be made to see that, in spite of his awe-inspiring energy and effort at control, "his inescapable limitations await him."[42] Repeatedly in the chapters of this last section we are told of the destruction and mutability that attend all Ahab's activities and indeed of the transience of all life. Ahab's leg, the book's central metaphor for this impermanence, itself breaks down again and again; several casks of oil in the *Pequod*'s hold inexplicably start leaking; even the robust Queequeg takes sick and comes to the edge of his grave; various other crewmembers die through accidents or fierce encounters with the whale; whaleboats are stove and, once repaired, stove again; the ship's compasses are permanently destroyed in a storm; the log line deteriorates and snaps; the life-buoy dries out and sinks.

Under the misguided command of the monomaniacal captain known as "*Old* Thunder" (92, 505; emphasis added), everything on ship runs to decay and disorder. Unlike the ageless thunder that speaks in the typhoon, Ahab is dying; his power inexorably "leaks" away (474). He has lost the power to deliver the lightning-bolt, symbol of spiritual illumination, that would free the heavenly waters and bring life-giving rain. While he never possessed this power in his own person, the potential was always there, waiting to operate through him, as it can through anyone. But since his dismemberment, Ahab has been so blinded by pride and the needs of his own ego as to be incapable of knowing the promise of divine grace within himself. Only the ever-renewing thunder of the true gods—the illusion-shattering energy of nature, of the whale speaking without, and of the soul speaking within—can restore one to life and keep life fresh in the midst of the decay that time inevitably brings. As described in "The Needle," chapter 124, it is this thunder that turns around the *Pequod*'s compasses on the night of the great storm and leads the crew to sail away from Moby Dick, toward safety, if only for a time.

"Ahab's Leg" places the *Pequod*'s captain in the tradition of the Fisher King, the ancient Mesopotamian figure that, as Jessie Weston argued in *From Ritual to Romance,* formed the basis of the medieval Christian Grail legend. Like the Fisher King, Ahab is a wounded ruler who seeks to restore his own health and potency by capturing a fish of miraculous revitalizing power.[43] Part human, part divine, he stands, like the early fertility cult figures of Osiris, Attis, and Adonis, between the people he commands and the mysterious forces that control his destiny. In several versions of the Grail story, there is a causal relation, as there is in *Moby-Dick,* between the vitality of the king and the health of his land or people: when he is vigorous, they know prosperity; but when his forces have been depleted or destroyed "by wound, sickness, old age, or death," as Weston says, "the land becomes waste, and the task of the hero is that of restoration." The Grail legend thus had its basis in early vegetation rituals or dramatized celebrations of the cycle of the seasons, running from birth through growth and decay and on to birth again.[44]

Because the foot, according to Freud, is an "age-old sexual symbol," Ahab's dismemberment can also be understood as a symbolic emasculation.[45] However, it is an emasculation that becomes almost literal in chapter 106, where Melville details the history of Ahab's trials with various replacements for his severed leg. On one occasion, which occurred on a night just before the ship sailed with Ishmael from Nantucket, Ahab had been discovered lying insensible on the ground with his ivory limb inexplicably broken loose and all but piercing his "groin." What makes Ahab unusual as an exemplar of the Fisher King is that his wounds are, to a significant degree, self-generated, even self-inflicted. As an epic writer of the nineteenth century, Melville provided a modern psychological rendering of the ritualistic sacrifice according to which Ahab, the ruling demigod, unconsciously contributes to his own destruction. He is not the victim of an arbitrary fate so much as he is his own worst enemy. As Ishmael makes the case at the start of "Ahab's Leg," where he describes the most recent instance of the limb's giving way under him, "The precipitating manner in which Captain Ahab had quitted the Samuel Enderby of London, had not been unattended with some small violence to his own person." So eager was he to get on with his mad chase after the White Whale that he gave his ivory leg "a half-splintering shock" when he leaped into his boat and then, after reaching the ship, did still further violence to it when in a fit of fury he "vehemently" turned to give an urgent command to the helmsman to pursue his course more "inflexibly" (463). A "hard-driver," as the carpenter calls him, who persists without caution in his pursuit of the Whale, Ahab thus becomes his own destroyer. He has "driven one leg to death, and spavined the other for life, and now wears out bone legs by the cord," in seemingly endless repetition of the universal fate (472).

In contrast to Ahab, who incarnates the will to destruction, the carpenter, the central figure in the next chapter, incarnates what Melville calls the "unaccountable, cunning life-principle" (468). Where the relentless Ahab destroys, with impunity, legs and anything else he has a mind to, the ship's carpenter humbly makes the repairs that keep the captain, and his men, functioning. In the face of "those thousand nameless mechanical emergencies continually recurring in a large ship," he represents the force that keeps all operations

from grinding to a halt, "repairing stove boats, sprung spars, reforming the shape of clumsy-bladed oars, inserting bull's eyes in the deck, or new tree-nails in the side planks" (466). Like a universal redeemer or practical savior (like Christ, also a humble carpenter), he seems able to prolong the life of mortal materials almost endlessly by refashioning them when they break down. Sixty years old or more himself, he is nonetheless "uncompromised as a new-born babe," his youthfulness a consequence of his lack of ego, for he lived "without premeditated reference to this world or the next." Unlike Ahab, he has no prideful sense of himself to protect and can thus maintain the attitude of "humorousness" he needs to carry him beyond the tragedy of loss and destruction (467–68). Unlike Ahab, the carpenter does not hold to a slanted, pessimistic view of grief; he does not believe, as Ahab does, that "both the ancestry and posterity of Grief go further than the ancestry and posterity of Joy" (464). Able to see beyond the limited tragic view of life, he doggedly persists in the cobbling, halfway measures—the refashioning of coffins into life-buoys—that can result in deliverance from the ravages of time and death. "Ahab's Leg" testifies to the hardness, pain, and brevity of life. But "The Carpenter" testifies to the truth that all mortality is balanced by an endlessly persistent and resourceful life energy.

Not everything, of course, can be forever repaired, as the old Manxman tries to tell Ahab later in "The Log and the Line." When a life finally breaks, there is no refashioning it; when it slips away, there is no carpenter's vise strong enough to hold it in place. One must, therefore, accept death as a new stage in existence, secure in the faith that the Father who makes all things knows what He is doing. Without such faith, even as he is without the knowledge of his own father, Ahab tries to resist the forces of death at the same time that he unconsciously courts them.

By contrast, Queequeg, Ishmael's spiritual guide, in "Queequeg in his Coffin" (chapter 110), shows himself to be as fearless of death as he is capable of conquering it. When a sizable leak is discovered in the *Pequod*'s hold, it is Queequeg who goes down to investigate the source of trouble. There, mysteriously, he is seized with a murderous fever that brings him "close to the very sill of the door of death." He thus becomes, in this chapter, an image of the adventurer going to his "endless end." Unlike Ahab, Queequeg shows no signs of egotism, and no possessiveness regarding his body. As his flesh wastes away "till there seemed but little left of him but his frame and tattooing," he does not rail against his fate, as Ahab does, or jealously guard his dwindling store of vitality. Instead, he accepts his fate, at the same time he grows more spiritual. His eyes "seemed growing fuller and fuller . . . a wondrous testimony to that immortal health in him which could not die, or be weakened" (476–77). By contrast, Ahab, on the last day of the chase, with Moby Dick bearing down on him for the last time, cries out that he grows "blind." "Is't night?" he exclaims in bewilderment (570).

Calmly accepting the fact of his imminent death, Queequeg quietly makes all of the arrangements for his own burial, unlike Ahab, who resists even the slightest suggestion that he might be mortal. When the appointed hour seems near, for instance, the Polynesian tells Ishmael he would like to be buried in a little "coffin-canoe" made of dark wood, just like the ones the deceased whalemen of Nantucket are placed in, and the ship's carpenter is instructed to make one especially for him (478). In fact, he faces the prospect of death in much the same spirit as he faces life, namely, as an adventure or journey. He already understands what Ishmael eventually comes to see, that even death is "only a launching into the region of the strange Untried; it is but the first salutation to the possibilities of the immense Remote, the Wild, the Watery, the Unshored" (486). When it comes time to make preparations for his projected journey to heaven, Queequeg asks that his coffin be provisioned with food and water and the iron from his harpoon, symbol of all phallic power and of his death-defying commitment to life. In contrast to Ahab, who gives up his spear, hurling it defiantly into Moby Dick at the very moment of his own death, Queequeg never loses faith in the hero's adventure or in the life-sustaining powers of the universe. Once his coffin-canoe is ready to receive him, he makes "trial of its comforts" and then, asking that little Yojo be placed on his chest, he at last pronounces it "'Rarmai' (it will do; it is easy)," a simple yet profound religious utterance that Queequeg seems about to make almost every minute of his life (479).

As Ishmael's guide, Queequeg is more than an examplar of the spiritually whole man confidently confronting his fate. In the end, he is an image of the hero's eventual triumph over death, of the potential for renewal, and of the hero's need to return to the human community with the life-restoring gift of his example. Here also Queequeg incarnates Ishmael's destiny. For Ishmael, too, will come to the verge of his "endless end," only to experience a miraculous deliverance and then return home to perform the sort of task typically required of the epic hero. When the Polynesian goes down in the *Pequod*'s hold to inspect the casks believed to be leaking sperm oil, it is as though he becomes infected with the mortality eating away at the barrels down there, the same mortality that is slowly destroying Ahab's vitality.

However, lying in his coffin "as if in a dream," Queequeg reacts in a way that suggests he overhears, and takes to heart, the heavenly ramblings of little Pip, who praises the Polynesian as one who "dies game," while the distraught cabin boy castigates himself for his cowardice. Before long, Queequeg unexpectedly recovers from his strange malady, his only explanation being that, "at a critical moment, he had just recalled a little duty ashore, which he was leaving undone; and therefore had changed his mind about dying." As Melville structures this scene, it is as though Pip, the incarnation of the infantile unconscious who, as Starbuck says, "brings heavenly vouchers of all our heavenly homes," gives utterance to Queequeg's unconscious knowledge of the special responsibility he bears as one of the chosen men of courage. Reminded by Pip of his own true character and calling, Queequeg is thus also reminded of his own extraordinary power. He is free as only the hero of the spiritual epic is free: "to live or die," he believes, "was a matter of his own sovereign will and pleasure." Certainly "mere sickness could not kill him: nothing but a whale, or a gale, or some violent, ungovernable, unintelligent destroyer of that sort," or so he says (479–80).

In the end, though, even Queequeg is destroyed by just such a destroyer. But having carved on the lid of his coffin a copy of all the "twisted tattooing" on his body, he bequeathes to Ishmael not only the mysterious duty he had left unfinished on shore but the means of carrying it out—namely, a complete theory of the heavens and the earth, in "hieroglyphic" form, and a "mystical treatise on the art of attaining truth" that "a departed prophet and seer" of Queequeg's native island had originally etched on his skin. That theory and treatise, though they remain "a riddle to unfold," have likewise been preserved in the "wondrous work in one volume" called *Moby-Dick* that Ishmael writes on his return from the dead (480–81). The duty, and the means of accomplishing it, are thus passed along to Melville's readers as well.

More than anywhere else in this book, Melville at this moment reveals that Queequeg, spiritually serene and without regard for himself, is the central wisdom figure, the key to *Moby-Dick*. Queequeg in his coffin is an image of the ultimate treasure in the epic hero's quest, a testimonial to the indestructibility of the soul, despite the body's infirmity. Unlike Ahab, who seeks always to assure himself of his physical immortality, Queequeg knows that the fate of the body is of no consequence in the journey of the soul, that preoccupation with the life of the body in fact blinds the eye to the more glorious life of the spirit. He knows what Ahab will not recognize, that the desire for physical immortality is misguided; that bodily dismemberment is of necessity the experience of living in time; and that the discovery of the soul, and its immortality, is mankind's greatest treasure.

In "The Pacific" (chapter 111), where the hunt for Moby Dick intensifies, the *Pequod* moves into a strangely spiritual realm where the "gently awful stirrings" of the rolling sea seem, as Ishmael says, the expression of "some hidden soul beneath." Here, in this tranquil ocean that Ishmael has dreamed of gazing on since his youth, "millions of mixed shades and shadows, drowned dreams, somnambulisms, reveries; all that we call lives and souls, lie dreaming, dreaming, still; tossing like slumberers in their beds" (482). Yet clearly they are evident only to the spiritual man. Ahab, who is committed only to the task of destroying his destroyer, sees or senses almost none of the spirituality of the South Sea. He is blind to what is truly indestructible. Ishmael explains that where almost anyone else would be inspired by the "eternal swells" of the Pacific to "own" the god of nature, Ahab is so preoccupied as to have "few thoughts of Pan" (483). Even later, in "The Gilder," when the *Pequod* penetrates into the heart of the soothing Japanese cruising ground, where the "tranquil beauty and brilliancy" of the ocean's surface makes the voyager forget "the tiger heart that pants beneath it," Ahab is only temporarily affected by such "gilding." For, explains Ishmael, speaking of the soothing scenes before Ahab and his crew, "if these secret golden keys did seem to open in him his own secret golden treasuries, yet did his breath upon them prove but tarnishing" (492). Ahab knows more of the unseen world than the jolly commander of the *Bachelor,* who proclaims "good-humoredly" that he does not believe in Moby Dick and shrugs off the loss of two of his men as of no consequence (494). But because he holds fast to what he has, resents every loss, and distrusts the powers that support all life, Ahab sees only a fraction of the unseen world that Queequeg and Ishmael and other spiritually minded characters such as Pip are capable of sensing.

"The Pacific," the last threshold chapter of Melville's epic, marks the *Pequod*'s entrance into the realm ruled by Moby Dick. It is the place where the quester finally meets the Father, where he comes home to God. As a symbol of the serenity of the redeemed soul—of Queequeg in his coffin, of Ishmael after his change of heart—the Pacific Ocean serves as a reminder that the object of the quest is spiritual, and the quester's proper attitude is one of faith, not anxiety, hostility, or pride.

Yet because Ahab is committed to the life of the ego and not of the soul, from this point on, as his purpose intensifies, his every move is seen to contribute to his self-destruction. In the several chapters that follow, Melville, using elaborate epic imagery, dramatizes his version of the classic argument concerning the causes of the tragic hero's downfall.[46] In chapters 112 and 113, "The Blacksmith" and "The Forge," where Ahab oversees the manufacture of the harpoon that he imagines to be infallible, he stakes his whole enterprise on the power of the "artificial fire," rather than the sun, to lead him to his prey. Baptizing the finished weapon in the name of the devil, Ahab thus underscores his determination to defy his Maker in every way possible rather than admit his dependence on Him. Yet as Melville implies, he should instead follow the example of reverence and trust that Ahab himself witnesses one evening in the scene described in "The Dying Whale" (chapter 116). There, after he and his crew have slain several whales, they watch as the last of them, slowly expiring, turns "his homage-rendering and invoking brow" toward the sun.

For a time, even Ahab is strangely affected by this instance of what, among dying sperm whales, is a common occurrence, acknowledging to himself that even at sea "life dies sunwards full of faith." But his suspicion soon returns and he concludes that it is vain for the dying whale to "seek intercedings with yon all-quickening sun," for it "only calls forth life, but gives it not again" (496–97). From here on, Ahab commits himself to a "prouder, if a darker faith," or nihilism. As the next chapter, "The Whale Watch," makes clear, while Ahab's ego still searches blindly for assurances of his immortality "on land and on sea," he has become so swallowed up by fear of his own death that he dreams again and again of hearses (410–11).

"The Whale Watch," chapter 117, shows Ahab moving more and more in a nighttime world, a sunless world of fears and premonitions of his own death. "The Quadrant," the next chapter, makes explicit his final rejection of the sun, and with it his refusal to acknowledge that, like every other living thing, he is a child of the great star. Until the scene described here, Ahab is said to have paid regular obeisance to the sun, taking his observation of it every day, with the ship's quadrant, to determine the latitude of his ship. However, now, in the glassy Japanese sea, the sun shines with such "nakedness of unrelieved radiance" as "the insufferable splendors of God's throne"; and Ahab, pretending to grow impatient with the hunt but secretly overpowered by the sun's sheer glory, swears that he will no longer permit it to serve as his "Pilot." "Thou tellest me truly where I *am*," he exclaims in frustration, "but canst thou cast the least hint where I *shall* be? Or canst thou tell where some other thing besides me is this moment living? Where is Moby Dick?" Again coming to the verge of real insight, Ahab again backs away. Rather than abandon his mad plan, he throws down the quadrant and tramples on it, swearing he will be guided by it no more. Rather than depend on an instrument that casts "man's eyes aloft to that heaven, whose live vividness but scorches him," Ahab says, "as these old eyes are even now scorched with thy light, O sun," he vows from that moment on to be guided only by "the level ship's compass" and the equally "level" log and line (500–501).

Before long, however, Ahab will discover the fallibility of these earthly instruments, as the compass, by a process described in "The Needle" (chapter 124), is discovered to be inverted by the thunder of the great Typhoon, and the log-line, as described in chapter 125, is found to be so weathered as to snap the first time the log and line is put into use. Once having made the pact to take the infernal Fedallah rather than the sun as his "pilot," Ahab finds more and more that nothing in the world will support him or his mission. Everything goes against him.

Ahab's renunciation of the sun is the turning point in his dying soul's journey and ushers in the crisis of the fifth and final part of Melville's epic novel. Toward evening of the same day on which he had trampled on the quadrant, "the direst of all storms," a Typhoon, bursts on the Japan Sea, stripping the *Pequod* of her sails and leaving the men helpless before its wrath (503). It is as though Ahab's sacrilege has so angered the gods as to cause them to lash out with a great tempest, though the tempest is in fact their most dramatic warning for him to turn back.

The night scene presented in "The Candles" (chapter 119) has a moody, otherwordly atmosphere in keeping with its mysterious, seemingly supernatural happenings. In the midst of the storm, the three masts and yardarms all suddenly burst into pallid flame. While all the crew stand together "enchanted" and in a reverent attitude, intuitively sensing, as Ishmael says, that "God's burning finger has been laid on the ship" (506), Ahab assumes a stance of boldest defiance. Grasping the ship's lightning rod with his hand—not in an effort to absorb the heavenly power that streams through it into himself but out of a vain determination to measure his own power against that of the deity—he swears to the inviolability of his own ego, declaring proudly, "In the midst of the personified impersonal, a personality stands here. Though but a point at best; whencesoe'er I came; wheresoe'er I go; yet while I earthly live, the queenly personality lives in me, and feels her royal rights." When the lightning suddenly flashes and the corpusants flare up to new heights, as though in response to this profane assertion of his independence, Ahab gleefully owns that the flame is his "fiery father." But at the end of his fierce soliloquy he vows nonetheless to worship his "sire" not with reverence but "defyingly" (507–08). Clearly, his feud is now beyond all reason and beyond any possibility of satisfaction; it is indeed "quenchless," as Ishmael had earlier said of it (179).

Blinded as Ahab is by his egomania, it is left to Starbuck to read all the signs of the storm and interpret its general meaning. Thus even before Ahab discovers in "The Needle" that the Typhoon's thunder had turned the *Pequod*'s compasses, forcing the ship away from an encounter with the White Whale, Starbuck understands that the gale, in blowing from the east, was blowing them away from Moby Dick. And he understands, when he witnesses the flame issuing from Ahab's harpoon "like a serpent's tongue," the reverse of the process whereby Ahab and Perth had put fire into it, that it symbolically speaks to them the deity's own gravest warning: "God, God is against thee, old man." Though Ahab tries, at the end of this grand scene, to quiet the fears of his awestruck crew by overpowering the harpoon's mysterious flame with his own breath, several of the crew run from him, as if he were a giant tree on a level plain during a hurricane, a tree "whose very height and strength but render it so much the more unsafe, because so much the more a mark of thunderbolts" (508).

Ishmael's choice of image, significant in itself as an expression of Melville's conception of tragic hubris, suggests that the pyrotechnics of this scene are intended as a heavenly warning to all on the *Pequod* to ready themselves for an imminent disaster. Turn around, the storm says; unless you are prepared, you will be destroyed by the great White Whale. What the thunder says in *Moby-Dick,* then, is what it has always said to the people of the world everywhere, whether in the mythologies of Zeus, Yahweh, or the Supreme Buddha: those who come to the Father in pride will be struck down, while those who come in true humility will know that His glory is the glory of the redeemed soul. Only those who come to Him without ego, as Ishmael does in the last chapters, where he seems little more than a disembodied voice, will see the Father and recognize Him to be one with the soul of humankind.

On the morning after the storm, the ocean rolls in mighty swells, and the brilliant sun, at once muffled and diffused, spreads its "emblazonings" everywhere, making the sea "a crucible of molten gold" (516). It is as though the same supernatural energy displayed in the lightning the night before has now been quieted and diffused, bathing the whole world in its glory. So compelling, so magnetic an attraction is it that even Ahab, the man of darkness, is moved to fix his gaze on its morning splendor. And when it is discovered that the storm has reversed the compass, Ahab is forced once again to take his bearings by the sun, thus tacitly acknowledging his dependence on it, even though just the day before he had vowed to steer his course with nothing but level, worldly instruments. After righting the ship's path, Ahab pushes on, ignoring or misreading the meaning of the many natural occurrences that warn him to turn back. But while he seems more determined than ever to pursue his fatal course, the debate regarding his mission, and the beliefs that undergird it, rages in his own mind more and more and plagues him with ever-greater intensity.

Ahab's interior debate is brought to the fore in "The Deck" (chapter 127), during his brief exchange with the carpenter, as the latter works at turning Queequeg's coffin into a replacement for the dried-out life-buoy. Every move of the carpenter's, in this chapter, seems to Ahab to raise the unsettling question of whether there is life beyond death, whether one has such a thing as an immortal soul. The scene opens with Ahab offhandedly observing that the coffin is lying near the ship's hatchway, "handy to the vault," in his mordant phrase. To him it symbolizes that there is no transcendence to another world, no life after death, only a simple drop into the crypt. But before long he finds that the carpenter's every move somehow unsettles him, either by suggesting the inescapability of death or by calling into question Ahab's certainty that all faith is vain. And as a consequence, Ahab banishes him from his sight. "Despatch! and get these traps out of my sight," he exclaims, pointing to various of the carpenter's belongings that seem to trick his imagination into changing his most fundamental beliefs (527–28).

Even so, deep down Ahab recognizes that the true source of all his unsettling thoughts is his own mind. Hearing the "rat-tat!" of the banished carpenter's mallet in the distance, and sensing in the sound the ticking of a clock that reminds him of his mortality, he laments, "Oh! how immaterial are all materials! What things real are there, but imponderable thoughts?" The chapter ends with Ahab wondering whether he should, in the formulation of his own beliefs, follow the example of the carpenter and try to change the coffin, "the very dreaded symbol of grim death," into "an immortality preserver," an imaginative feat that he might be able to accomplish if he could somehow bring himself to believe in the immortality of the soul. Though he immediately dismisses such a possibility with the admission "so far gone am I in the dark side of earth," he nonetheless is made so nervous by the sounds of the carpenter as to feel driven to escape below deck (528). The scene ends ironically, with Ahab seeking Pip, the book's central image of the lost soul and the emblem of what Ahab refuses to acknowledge in himself. Such vacillation, sometimes unconscious, sometimes startlingly conscious, shows the *Pequod*'s captain to be a more fully rounded character than is generally recognized—not a simple madman with a monomaniacal hunger for revenge, but a deeply divided figure whose fixed purpose hides a profound distrust of the mercy of the Father and a fear that he himself might not be worthy.

In the remaining chapters leading up to the final chase, Melville devotes most of his effort to demonstrating that, "stricken, blasted, if he be," as Peleg had earlier told Ishmael, "Ahab has his humanities!" (79). If we are to see Ahab as more than a monster of rage, if we are to feel genuine sympathy for him, we must be made to recognize that his singlemindedness has cost him dearly, and we have to be made to understand that he himself appreciates what he has had to give up in so relentlessly pursing his one object. At the same time, we have to be made to see that Ahab's failure, in the end, is a failure of love, and that he manages to catch at least a glimpse of this idea on his own. In three scenes—Ahab's brief meeting with Captain Gardner of the *Rachel* in chapter 128; his poignant exchange with Pip in chapter 129; and his fluctuating discourse with Starbuck in "The Symphony," chapter 132—Ahab's fixedness of purpose is put to a series of profound tests.

In the first, when an acquaintance from Nantucket, the captain of the *Rachel,* comes aboard the *Pequod* and entreats Ahab to help him search for his lost son, Ahab seems to be completely unmoved by the man's plea. But when he suddenly orders Captain Gardiner from his ship, to prevent him from delaying his own search for Moby Dick, he reveals not only that he feels for his fellow captain but also that he knows he is committing a sin against his own soul. "God bless ye, man," he exclaims, "and may I forgive myself" (532).

In the second scene, Pip, who sees in Ahab's sturdy hand a "man-rope," something "weak souls may hold by" (522), asks nothing more than that he be permitted to accompany his captain wherever he goes on the ship. Ahab, however, finds Pip's fidelity "too curing to my malady." The desire to respond with a fidelity of his own would lead him, he knows, to give up the hunt for the Whale, and so he refuses even this seemingly trifling request. Still, Ahab is so deeply moved by the cabin boy's plea that he confesses his own purpose "keels up in him" unless Pip stops, and he finally has to threaten him with "murder" to make him leave (534).

In the third scene, when the first mate catches Ahab in an unprecedented mood of wistfulness and urges him one last time to turn back to Nantucket and their wives and children, Ahab shows himself suddenly of a mind to protect Starbuck, the only man on the *Pequod* who had ever openly opposed him, by encouraging him to stay on board when they give chase to Moby Dick. In this way, Starbuck might survive the confrontation with the Whale and return to his family. Momentarily moved by Starbuck's enthusiasm at the prospect of returning home, Ahab suddenly stops to wonder, with an air of all but unprecedented detachment, what it is that makes him persist in his quest for the White Whale. Using terms that bring him to the verge of defining his dilemma for himself for the first time, he nonetheless fails to recognize that his conflict is so deeply human as to be universal, a battle between sheer ego and the will to love. "What is it," he pleads with Starbuck, "what nameless, inscrutable, unearthly thing is it; what cozening, hidden lord and master, and cruel, remorseless emperor commands me; that against all natural lovings and longings, I so keep pushing, and crowding, and jamming myself on all the time; recklessly making me ready to do what in my own proper, natural heart, I durst not so much as dare?" (545).

Ahab cannot love because he cannot conquer his ego, and he cannot conquer his ego because he cannot bring himself to admit there is an "invisible power" that rules over all. Though he senses that his own heart could not beat nor his brain think "unless God does that beating, does that thinking, does that living, and not I," he is so jealous of his own power, so egotistical, that he is incapable of seeing humanity as being ruled by anything more than "Fate" (545). He may possess the potential, but Ahab is far from being the epic hero. Preoccupied more and more with the subjects of sleep and death in these late chapters, Ahab lacks the comprehensive understanding of the true hero, the kind that only the awakened soul can attain.

When seen for the first time early in "The Symphony," Ahab had been leaning over the side, not studying his own reflection, like Narcissus, but watching "how his shadow in the water sank and sank to his gaze," as though he were watching his own soul drown before his very eyes. At the end of the chapter, he is seen for the last time, before the three-day chase, in much the same position. After Starbuck has stolen away in despair, Ahab crosses the deck to gaze over the other side. But this time, instead of seeing his own image, he sees only the reflection of Fedallah, who is there leaning over the same rail. Only Ahab's shadow, the shade or ghost of his soul, and not the soul itself, survives in him now. Immediately at the start of the chase in the next chapter, then, Ahab is referred to as "the old man," one sign among many that he will soon be in his last death throes (543).

Death is the great subject of *Moby-Dick,* death and immortality. Nowhere is this more apparent than in the final section of Melville's epic, where to read of Ahab's quickening pursuit of the White Whale is to witness a man rushing, uncontrollably, into the jaws of destruction. More and more as the *Pequod* moves toward its inevitable confrontation with Moby Dick, it is as though it travels in a realm of death, a wasteland or place of trial, where men disappear or perish without a trace, the young and innocent as well as the seasoned and hearty. As they near the outskirts of the equatorial fishing grounds, on the line closest to the sun, Ishmael's shipmates hear cries just before dawn, cries that sound like the voices of "newly drowned men," as the old Manxman explains (523). At sunrise the next morning, the *Pequod* loses one of its own men when he falls from aloft, a premonition of the many sacrifices to come. And on the following day, they encounter the *Rachel,* whose captain has lost a son and other men as well while hunting the White Whale.

As evidenced by the example of the *Rachel,* and also of the *Delight,* the simple act of sighting Moby Dick can cost a sailor his life. "Hast seen the White Whale?" Ahab cries out to the *Rachel,* the word "seen" here taking on the meaning of a religious experience. "Aye, yesterday. Have ye seen a whale-boat adrift?" comes the ominous reply, as if there were some fatal connection between the act of beholding the great Whale and the sacrifice of a human life. Indeed, the waters inhabited by Moby Dick can be murderous to all but the chosen few. To the five men of the *Delight* who lost their lives to Moby Dick just hours before the *Pequod* crossed its path, the surrounding sea is indeed a sailors' "tomb," the burial place of the dead. Yet, with the exception of Ahab, those who survive an encounter with the Whale are usually quick to develop a healthy respect for the beast and to turn their thoughts to whatever prospects they might have for life in the next world. For them, a deadly sea can become a place of trial leading to eternal life. As the men of the *Delight* set about burying the one sailor recovered from the previous day's carnage, the captain voices a faith in "the resurrection and the life" that is never heard on the decks of Ahab's ship (541).

The waters inhabited by the great White Whale are the waters of life as well as of death. But to a man such as Ahab, whose pride corrodes all faith, they will never bring renewal. As symbolized by the loss of his hat, or crown, in chapter 130, Ahab is a dying king who is fast losing his power to rule, a type of the Fisher King for whom the living waters will never flow again. On the eve of the first day of the chase, Ahab is preoccupied with his weakness and his age, confessing to Starbuck that he feels "deadly faint" with his burden and "intolerably old," and he even jests that his gray hair must have grown "from out some ashes." Having spent forty years at sea making war on the horrors of the deep, he comes at last to recognize that his life is an emptiness, that he has failed to gain anything of true value. Unlike Moses, whose forty-year trial was eventually rewarded with the discovery of the Promised Land, Ahab wonders now at the end of his time how he might be "the richer or better" for all his struggle and concludes bitterly that he has been "a forty years' fool." For all his adult years he has suffered privation, knowing almost nothing but the solitary life of a whaling captain and feeding "upon dry salted fare—fit emblem," as he tells his first mate, "of the dry nourishment of my soul" (543–44).

Yet only when Ahab sheds a lone tear as he stands gazing into the sea and muses over all he has missed on shore these many years—human sympathy, friendship and family life, the green world—is it clear that he understands the many sacrifices he has had to make. And only then is it clear that he is worthy of our attention and sympathy, that he is fully human, capable of appreciating the common life, and that he feels as we feel. "Nor did all the Pacific contain such wealth as that one wee drop," Ishmael says, for that one drop symbolizes a human soul lost (543–44). More than a sentimental touch, this one tear signals Ahab's one moment of complete self-understanding. Though he will not turn back even now, his tear of self-knowledge symbolizes the "freeing of the waters," to appropriate Jesse Weston's phrase, the release of the life-giving rain or pent-up rivers into the dying world, and the washing away of death and evil and egotism that holds the wasteland in its grip.[47] Before the "great shroud of the sea" can roll on, restored to its equilibrium of five-thousand years before, it must unleash the havoc that will right the disequilibrium brought about by Ahab's immense pride (572).

The three-day chase, powerfully suspenseful though it is as drama, brings no significant surprises for the reader, only a resounding resolution, the most perfect an epic novelist has ever imagined. When at dawn of the first day Ahab senses Moby Dick's proximity and orders Daggoo to "Call all hands!" the black harpooneer wakes the sleeping crew with great thundering "judgment claps" on the forecastle deck, as if summoning them all to their final reckoning (547). Clearly, when judgment is pronounced, Ahab will be found guilty of refusing the call to adventure, the call to bring his will into line with the divine will. Clearly, he and his men are doomed. Yet even at this late hour, Ahab is free, in the way Milton's Satan was free, to decide to live eternally or die; even at this late hour, Ahab holds his fate in his own hands, even as he holds the spear, the masculine symbol of life and instrument of death known from the Grail legend and elsewhere, that will determine his destiny. In *Moby-Dick* the epic question—is humankind fated or free?—returns with the return of the Whale in the book's waning moments and is here resolved once and for all. Melville shows not simply that Ahab's life is taken from him but that Ahab himself, refusing to take life on any terms other than his own misguided ones, deliberately, willfully, tragically gives it up, even as he gives up his harpoon. Although the *Pequod*'s captain, after the nearly fatal second day of the chase, lectures Starbuck that he cannot turn around and head for home, his claim that "This whole act's immutably decreed . . . I am the Fates' lieutenant" is a sign of the advanced state of his *amor fati,* the failed hero's fatal love of fate that masks his yearning to be free of all personal accountability for his actions (561–62). As Ahab had confessed only moments earlier, while being lifted into the *Pequod* after his ivory leg had broken one more time, "Aye, aye, Starbuck, 'tis sweet to lean sometimes" (560). Here, too, he finds it comforting to shift the burden of responsibility for the coming destruction away from himself and to give it instead to the mysterious Fates.

Not until Ahab finally gives up his harpoon, not once but three times, thrusting it into the Whale in his ultimate act of defiance, does the beast turn on him with all its fury. On the first day's chase, Moby Dick simply toys with Ahab's boat, "as a mildly cruel cat her mouse" (550); afterward, an exhausted Ahab desperately asks whether the harpoon is "safe," and he is told by Stubb, "Aye, sir, for it was not darted." Significantly, after making anxious inquiries, Ahab learns also that his crew is safe as well, and for the same reason, namely, the harpoon was not thrown. Significantly, too, Ahab himself, though only moments earlier he had been lying "all crushed" in the bottom of Stubb's boat, quickly revives, "the eternal sap" running up in his bones again (551–52). On the second day it becomes more evident still that the harpoon is a magical instrument, its misuse a crime punishable by death. This time, on learning

that Fedallah is missing, Ahab is forced to recall that he had thrown his iron into Moby Dick in their last encounter. And on the third day the pattern is consummated. Ahab is destroyed, but not until he has darted two more spears into the White Whale and turned his own body, as he says emphatically, away "from the sun" (571). No sooner does he plunge the last of these instruments into his foe than he is caught around the neck by the whaleline and dragged under, a victim, like the Parsee, of Ahab's own weapon. Three times he was given the chance to choose life rather than death, and three times he chose to give up the spear in hatred and defiance. Having failed the test not once but three times, his fate is sealed: he deserves to live no more.

Whether Ishmael, more than any of the rest of the *Pequod*'s crew, deserves to live—more than Queequeg, say, or Pip—is the book's crowning mystery, its lone unanswered question. Ahab's fate is predictable. Even the destruction of all the ship's crew comes as no surprise. The great mystery for Melville, in the end, is not death but life, the unfathomable gratuitousness of it. The "Epilogue," brief yet dense, a little treasure that radically alters the meaning of all the rest of the book, conveys nothing so strongly as Ishmael's own wonder at his continued existence, at his survival of the wrath of the avenging God. Only the slightest attempt is made to explain his escape. All we are told is that "the Fates ordained" that he would be the one called on to assume Fedallah's place in Ahab's boat on the third day of the chase, after the Parsee had gone down with the Whale. From there, it just happened that, of the three oarsmen tossed out of the boat on the next encounter with Moby Dick, Ishmael was the one who was left a castaway, floating beyond the reach of the White Whale's final frenzy. Otherwise, the fact that he alone was specially chosen is presented as a matter beyond human understanding.

Not only did he survive the wrath of Moby Dick and the awful power of the sinking *Pequod*'s whirlpool, but he has also somehow been preserved from the universal cannibalism of the sea. For "one whole day and night" Ishmael is mysteriously protected from the sharks, who "glided by as if with padlocks on their mouths," and from the "savage sea-hawks," who "sailed with sheathed beaks," before he is finally plucked out of the sea by the *Rachel* (573). A lone man somehow persisting in a hostile universe, buoyed up on a miniature version of the world we all inhabit—part life-buoy, part coffin—Ishmael in the end is an image of us all, gifted with life and miraculously surviving, moment by moment.

An everyman figure, Ishmael is also, paradoxically, the specially chosen one. He alone is the universal epic hero of *Moby-Dick*. Though an orphan and outcast, lacking family, wealth, and other conventional forms of legitimacy, he is the one man on the ill-fated *Pequod* whose cry God hears. Indeed, his name, the name he takes for himself, means "God shall hear." This is the identity he discovers for himself at the climax of his adventure: the one whom God hears. "Ishmael" is not the given name of Melville's narrator; it is the name he appropriates for himself after the fact, because it so aptly captures his experience as a castaway who in the end finds the Father after all. Like other epic stories, therefore, Ishmael's story climaxes with the discovery of the hero's true character and ends with his return to the community of his birth to bear witness to what he has learned. His retelling of that story, in turn, begins with the famous line that announces his identity: "Call me Ishmael." It is the vitalizing declaration of a man who knows from personal experience that God and the soul of the redeemed hero are one.

His identity having been revealed to him in the moment of his soul's greatest test, Ishmael returns to share the wealth of his discovery with the people of his own land, those Sunday "water-gazers" of Manhattan, and elsewhere, who long for the adventure that will liberate the soul.[48] This wealth or treasure is contained within the pages of *Moby-Dick,* the book that records its hero's experience on the *Pequod* and bodies forth the wisdom Ishmael has gained from the events leading up to the fateful confrontation with the Whale. Ishmael does not, of course, capture the White Whale with a harpoon, as Ahab would try to do. Being divine, Moby Dick can never be taken that way. But Ishmael can be said to capture him with his pen in the book called *The Whale* with potentially life-changing consequences to his readers.

Not the Whale, but the grace the Whale embodies—this is what the hero must seek. The Whale's "grace" cannot be destroyed, as Ahab would have it, for it is of the very essence of life; and life, we know from Melville's tale, is the abiding, indestructible mystery. When we read *Moby-Dick,* we have the chance to partake of that grace, if we can bring ourselves to take up the call. Those of us who read Melville's book and discover thereby something of our deeper selves are like the redeemed of Yahweh who, as Campbell says, are "served the inexhaustible, delicious flesh of the monsters Behemoth, Leviathan, and Ziz" at the Messianic banquet.[49] Going into Melville's epic, into the belly of *The Whale,* we find not that we are contained or trapped there but that we are fed and sustained. *Moby-Dick,* that is to say, is more than the story of one man's renewal. It is that still rarer thing, a religious text, a world-redeeming epic.

Notes

1. While I feel obliged to follow Melville's public testimony here, I suspect Harrison Hayford's theory is right: "Melville wrote the essay not before but after he met Hawthorne." See Hayford's dissertation, "Melville and Hawthorne: A Biographical and Critical Study" 69.

2. Melville, "Hawthorne and His Mosses" 253.

3. Still, the number who have featured the subject of the epic are surprisingly small. In addition to Arvin's "The Whale" (in *Herman Melville*) and Pommer's "Poetic and Epic Influences of *Paradise Lost*" (in *Milton and Melville*), these include just two essays, both from the previous decade: Lord's "The Ivory *Pequod* and the Epic of Illusion" and McWilliams's "Till a Better Epic Comes Along." Two essays from the 1970s that would seem especially pertinent, Slotkin's "*Moby-Dick:* The American National Epic" (in *Regeneration through Violence*) and Rosenberry's "Epic Romance: *Moby-Dick*" (in *Melville*), in fact offer little discussion of Melville's novel as an epic per se.

4. See Hutson and McCoy 9ff.

5. See Franklin, *The Wake of the Gods.*

6. As seen in his letter of June 1[?], 1851, to Hawthorne, written while finishing *Moby-Dick,* Melville doubted that his effort would be appreciated, but his mistrust masks his intention: "What's the use of elaborating what, in its very essence, is so short-lived as a modern book? Tho I wrote the Gospels in this century, I should die in the gutter." See Leyda 1:411. In a recent study that indirectly supports my own view, Lawrence Buell has argued that Melville's novel can be read as an instance of scripture; see his "*Moby-Dick* as Sacred Text."

7. See Abercrombie; Cook; and Newman.

8. Campbell, *The Hero with a Thousand Faces* 30.

9. Eliade, "Initiation and the Modern World" esp. 115. Eliade here distinguishes among three types of initiation: puberty rites, initiation into secret societies, and shamanic initiations. These last two both involve the "deepening of the religious experience and knowledge," even to the point of a "death" and "resurrection" wherein the initiate emerges in a new form, namely, as a spiritual being. Shamanic initiations are reserved for teachers or medicine men and "consist in ecstatic experiences (e.g., dreams, visions, trances) and in an instruction imparted by the spirits or the old

master shamans (e.g., shamanic techniques, names and functions of the spirits, mythology and genealogy of the clan, secret language)." I see Ishmael's initiation as combining these last two types—initiation into the whaling fraternity and into the ways and knowledge of the shaman or "consecrated individual" (114–16).

10. See Campbell, *Hero with a Thousand Faces* 15.

11. Merchant, in his survey of the form, argues that, while *The Waste Land* lacks the "discursive variety of epic," it has "many features in common" with it and with modern poetic versions of the genre such as Ezra Pound's *Cantos* (92). Because it lacks the amplitude of the true epic, however, Eliot's poem qualifies technically only as a "mini-epic."

12. Abercrombie 16.

13. Eliot, *The Waste Land* 67, l. 431.

14. For an illuminating study of Ishmael as a survivor of an apocalyptic catastrophe, like the survivors of the Holocaust, see the work of my former student, Janet Reno.

15. *Moby-Dick* 3. Subsequent references to *Moby-Dick* are to the Hayford, Parker, and Tanselle edition.

16. Campbell, *Hero with a Thousand Faces* 29.

17. Ibid. 69–73.

18. Note that Mapple's description of Jonah's escape route calls attention to the fact that the Mediterranean is shaped like a whale, thus symbolically conveying the idea that Jonah can be said to be already in the "belly of the whale" even at the moment when he is trying to flee God (43).

19. Cf. "The Lamp," chapter 97, one of many instances of this image that appear throughout *Moby-Dick*.

20. Cf. Melville's remark in his June 1[?], 1851, letter to Hawthorne, written while completing *Moby-Dick:* "The reason the mass of men fear God, and *at bottom dislike* Him, is because they rather distrust His heart, and fancy Him all brain like a watch." See Davis and Gilman, eds., 128–29.

21. This is an early example of the displacement of roles and multiplication of characters typically found in epics, where themes are built up through variation and duplication to create the effects of richness and resonance, of plenitude and depth, and where indirection is necessarily the overriding method. Virtually everything in *Moby-Dick* is presented indirectly, rather than directly, as if seen in a mirror: Jonah's story is seen through Mapple's eyes; Mapple's story through Ishmael's; even Ishmael's story is presented not as it happens but after the fact, namely, "now that I recall all the circumstances," as he says (7), or after he has had time to reflect on it. It is, of course, in the nature of all literature to work by indirection. But in an epic it is among the chief techniques the poet has at his disposal for generating the sense of heft or weight so characteristic of the genre. In effect, it creates a "double" sense of the subject and thus gives it "double" weight. Thus, the hundreds of instances of "doubling" in the opening chapters of *Moby-Dick* that Harrison Hayford has brought together in his illuminating essay, "Unnecessary Duplicates: A Key to the Writing of *Moby-Dick,*" are not evidences of Melville's failure to edit out the early version of his book from the final one, as Hayford argues. Instead, I believe they are evidences of Melville's epic intentions, some of them, such as the famous tiller that turns into a wheel, presumably playful or ironic in intent.

22. Cf. "The Pipe," chapter 30, where Ahab, finding that his pipe "no longer soothes," tosses it into the sea (129).

23. Tillyard 15–16. As illuminating as I find Tillyard's theoretical statements about the epic, I do not agree with his view that *Moby-Dick* fails to qualify as an example of the form. Tillyard argues that Melville's narrative is a "great book" but that it is not "choric." However, if we take Ishmael to be the central hero, rather than Ahab, and define the group Ishmael is speaking for not simply as rude whalemen but as "modern democratic man [and woman]," or "the American at midcentury," I believe the book qualifies even on this count, as well as on many others.

24. Abercrombie 16–17.

25. See Winnifrith; and Newman 20–21.

26. Abercrombie 68–69.

27. Merchant 27.

28. Campbell, *Hero with a Thousand Faces* 15.

29. See ibid. 59–60.

30. See ibid. 101.

31. Ibid. 25, 40ff.

32. Campbell appropriates the term from Nicholas of Cusa, in *De visione Dei,* as cited by Anada K. Coomaraswamy, "On the One and Only Transmigrant," in *Supplement to the Journal of the American Oriental Society* (April-June, 1944): 25.

33. Campbell, *Hero with a Thousand Faces* 109–11.

34. The *Pequod*'s first whale sighting is described at the end of "The Mat-Maker," but in response to Tashtego's cry of "There she blows!" Ishmael "gaz[es] up at the clouds whence that voice dropped like a wing" (215). Even while standing watch, he confesses, he "kept but sorry guard" (158). And, as we are told here, he has his back to the whale, even when he is in close proximity and in hot pursuit. Until the very end, he is never in a position to see a live whale close up and out of the water; and, as he explains elsewhere, seeing a dead whale out of the water is a very different matter.

35. See Davis and Gilman, eds., 78. Quotations from Emerson 35.

36. Campbell, *Hero with a Thousand Faces* 118.

37. In substituting the whale's head for its "belly" in the mythical journey of the hero, Melville might be said to have subscribed to the view of one Bishop Jebb, who had once defended the truth of Jonah's story on the grounds that "it is not necessary . . . that we consider Jonah as entombed in the whale's belly, but as temporarily lodged in some part of his mouth." The distinction, of course, does not much matter, finally, given the metaphoric character of Melville's writing generally in this narrative. In this same chapter, "Jonah Historically Regarded," Melville even suggests that the "whale" in the biblical story might have been nothing more than a ship of that name or, more outrageously, a "life-preserver—an inflated bag of wind—which the endangered prophet swam to, and so was saved from a watery doom" (364–65).

38. "A Squeeze of the Hand" is thus also an instance of the bath motif, found especially in oral epics and discussed recently by Foley at some length, along with the greeting and feast motifs, in connection with the *Odyssey* (248–57). As both Foley and Arend point out, this theme includes "washing, annointing, and donning new clothes," a combination of activities that makes Melville's juxtaposition of "A Squeeze of the Hand" and "The Cassock," chapters 94 and 95, especially significant.

39. Campbell, *Hero with a Thousand Faces* 145.

40. See M. H. Abrams.

41. See Campbell, *Hero with a Thousand Faces* 40–41; see also Eliade, *The Sacred and the Profane* 42–47.

42. See Greene 15–18.

43. The only previous discussion of the *Pequod*'s captain as an exemplar of the Fisher King is Dow, "Ahab: The Fisher King."

44. Weston 13, 24.

45. Freud, *Three Essays* 21.

46. As Newman has pointed out, tragedy has always been closely associated with epic, Homer being credited with the invention of both forms (15). See also Ker 16; and Greene 16.

47. Weston 13.

48. In this respect, I have to disagree with McWilliams's conclusion, in "Till A Better Epic Comes Along," that *Moby-Dick* departs from the paradigm of Campbell's "monomyth" by failing to develop the third stage, or "return," and neglecting to define a community "to which the tale may be recounted" (203, 209). Though in general I find McWilliams's discussion to be both apt and illuminating, I would argue instead that the "return" stage is defined mainly by the period of Ishmael's composition of *Moby-Dick* and that his tale is intended for the whole community of Americans he left on land in the beginning of his narrative. More generally, however, all of the book's landlocked readers the world over could be said to constitute the "community" to which the story is directed.

49. Campbell, *Hero with a Thousand Faces* 177.

Bibliography

Abercrombie, Lascelles. *The Epic.* 1914. Freeport, NY: Books for Libraries Press, 1969.

Abrams, M. H. *The Mirror and the Lamp: Romantic Theory and the Critical Tradition.* 1953. New York: Norton, 1958.

Arend, Walter. *Die typischen Scenen bei Homer.* Berlin: Weidmann, 1933.

Arvin, Newton. *Herman Melville.* New York: William Sloan, 1950.

Buell, Lawrence. "*Moby-Dick* as Sacred Text." *New Essays on Moby-Dick.* Ed. Richard H. Brodhead. Cambridge: Cambridge UP, 1986. 53–72.

Campbell, Joseph. *The Hero with a Thousand Faces.* 1949. Princeton: Princeton UP, 1968.

Cook, Albert. *The Classic Line: A Study of Epic Poetry.* Bloomington: Indiana UP, 1966.

Davis, Merrell R., and William H. Gilman, eds. *The Letters of Herman Melville.* New Haven: Yale UP, 1960.

Dow, Janet. "Ahab: The Fisher King." *Connecticut Review* 2 (April 1969): 42–49.

Eliade, Mircea. "Initiation and the Modern World." *The Quest: History and Meaning in Religion.* Chicago: U of Chicago P, 1969. 112–26.

———. *The Sacred and the Profane: The Nature of Religion.* Trans. Willard R. Trask. New York: Harcourt, 1959.

Eliot, T. S. *The Waste Land.* 1922. In *T. S. Eliot: Selected Poems.* New York: Harcourt, 1964.

Foley, John Miles. *Traditional Oral Epic: The Odyssey, Beowulf, and the Serbo-Croatian Return Song.* Berkeley: U of California P, 1990.

Franklin, H. Bruce. *The Wake of the Gods: Melville's Mythology.* Stanford: Stanford UP, 1963.

Freud, Sigmund. *Three Essays on the Theory of Sexuality.* Trans. James Strachey. New York: Basic Books, 1962.

Greene, Thomas. *The Descent from Heaven: A Study in Epic Continuity.* New Haven: Yale UP, 1963.

Hayford, Harrison. "Melville and Hawthorne: A Biographical and Critical Study." Ph.D. diss. Yale University, 1945.

———. "Unnecessary Duplicates: A Key to the Writing of *Moby-Dick*." *New Perspectives on Melville*. Ed. Faith Pullin. Kent, OH: Kent State UP, 1978. 128–61.

Hutson, Arthur E., and Patricia McCoy. "General Introduction." *Epics of the Western World*. Philadelphia: Lippincott, 1954. 7–15.

Ker, W. P. *Epic and Romance: Essays on Medieval Literature*. 1896. London: Macmillan, 1926.

Leyda, Jay. *The Melville Log: A Documentary Life of Herman Melville, 1819–1891*. 2 vols. 1951. Rpt. with a new supplement. New York: Gordian Press, 1969.

Lord, George de Forest. "The Ivory *Pequod* and the Epic of Illusion." *Trials of the Self: Heroic Ordeals in the Epic Tradition*. Hamden, CT: Archon Books, 1983. 157–91.

McWilliams, John P., Jr. "Till a Better Epic Comes Along." *The American Epic: Transforming a Genre, 1770–1860*. Cambridge: Cambridge UP, 1989. 187–216.

Melville, Herman. "Hawthorne and His Mosses." 1850. Rpt. in *The Piazza Tales and Other Prose Pieces, 1839–1860*. Ed. Harrison Hayford, Alma A. MacDougall, and G. Thomas Tanselle. Evanston, IL: Northwestern UP/Newberry Library, 1987.

———. *Moby-Dick: or The Whale*. Ed. Harrison Hayford, Hershel Parker, and G. Thomas Tanselle. Evanston, IL: Northwestern UP/Newberry Library, 1988.

Merchant, Paul. *The Epic*. London: Methuen, 1971.

Newman, John Kevin. *The Classical Epic Tradition*. Madison: U of Wisconsin P, 1986.

Pommer, Henry F. *Milton and Melville*. Pittsburgh: U of Pittsburgh P, 1950.

Reno, Janet. *Ishmael Alone Survived*. Lewisburg, PA: Bucknell UP, 1990.

Rosenberry, Edward H. *Melville*. Boston: Routledge and Kegan Paul, 1979.

Slotkin, Richard. "*Moby-Dick:* The American National Epic." *Regeneration through Violence: The Mythology of the American Frontier, 1600–1860*. Middletown, CT: Wesleyan UP, 1973. 538–50.

Tillyard, E. M. W. *The Epic Strain in the English Novel*. London: Chatto and Windus, 1958.

Weston, Jessie L. *From Ritual to Romance*. 1920. New York: Peter Smith, 1941.

Winnifrith, Tom. "Postscript." *Aspects of the Epic*. Ed. Tom Winnifrith, Penelope Murray, and K. W. Grandsden. London: Macmillan, 1983. 109–18.

Index

Sounding the Whale

~

was composed in 10/13 Minion
on a Gateway 2000 PC
using PageMaker for Windows
at The Kent State University Press;
printed by The Collier Printing Company;
designed by Will Underwood;
and published by

~

The Kent State University Press
Kent, Ohio 44242